Fruitful Hands

By Jacquelynne Steves

Fruitful Hands By Jacquelynne Steves

Editor: Donna di Natale
Designer: Bob Deck
Photography: Aaron T. Leimkueler
Watercolor art and diagrams: Jacquelynne Steves
Illustration: Eric Sears
Technical Editor: Kathe Dougherty
Production assistance: JoAnn Groves
Food styling and photography by Chris Steves and Jacquelynne Steves

Published by:
Kansas City Star Books
1729 Grand Blvd.
Kansas City, Missouri, USA 64108

First edition, first printing
ISBN: 9781935362890

Library of Congress Control Number: 2011928999
Printed in the United States of America by Walsworth Publishing Co., Marceline, MO

To order copies, call StarInfo at (816) 234-4636 and say "Books."

Table of Contents

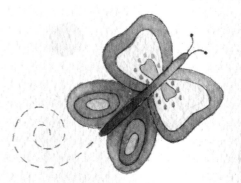

About the Author

Jacquelynne has been creative all her life. Her collection of hobbies includes painting with watercolors and acrylics, sewing quilts and clothing, cross stitch, embroidery, punch needle, paper crafts, photography, going to flea markets, home decorating, and getting creative in the kitchen. She loves living a creative life in a 160-year-old farmhouse with her husband and two daughters. When not sewing, painting, or cooking something, she can be found in the garden, at her church singing and volunteering, or spending time at the beach with her family.

She also thoroughly enjoys being the owner/designer of The Noble Wife pattern company and a fabric designer for Henry Glass Fabrics. You can visit her website at **www.TheNobleWife.com** and her blog at **www.TheNobleWife.blogspot.com**.

DEDICATION

To the women in my life who were creative by necessity, and led the way for my own creative legacy:

My mother, Gloria Jean Pellegrini Jost, who could always make something out of nothing, be it a wonderful meal from whatever was in the refrigerator, or cute Halloween decorations made from construction paper.

My maternal grandmother, Margaret Ridgeway Pellegrini, who taught me to sew and crochet, and took me with her to ceramics classes.

My paternal grandmother, Clara Fisher Jost, who did not know what it was like to live without a garden full of flowers, fruits and vegetables.

Acknowledgments

Thanks to my family for always believing in me, even when (and *especially* when) I didn't believe in myself.

Thanks to my editor Donna diNatale, book designer Bob Deck, and to Diane McLendon and everyone behind the scenes at Kansas City Star who have worked so hard to bring this project to completion and who have made the publication of my first book such an enjoyable experience.

Thanks to Harriet Clemens at Henry Glass Fabrics, who "discovered" me at a Quilt Market a couple of years ago and has been a wonderful source of encouragement in my professional journey.

Thanks to Brenda Riddle of Acorn Quilt and Gift Company, who has always been so kind to me and so generous with her advice.

Thanks to Granite Transitions for allowing us to photograph the projects in this book at their beautiful showroom in Lenexa, Kansas.

Enormous gratitude and humble thankfulness to God for any gifts and talents that I might possess, and for the opportunity to live a creative life and share it with others.

And, thanks to *everyone* who has either purchased this book or one of my patterns or my fabric, read my blog, or sent me kind words of encouragement, your validation and support means more to me than you can ever know. I thank you from the bottom of my heart.

CREDITS

The Citrus Peel Quilt was pieced and appliqued by Jacquelynne Steves and machine quilted by Kathleen Johnson of Gwenevere and Me Quilting.

The House on a Hill Quilt was pieced, embroidered and appliqued by Jacquelynne Steves and machine quilted by Alison Luff.

The Walk Around the Block Quilt was pieced by Alison Luff, appliquéd by Jacquelynne Steves, and machine quilted by Alison Luff.

All other projects in this book were completed by Jacquelynne Steves.

SOURCES

DMC: Embroidery floss. www.dmc-usa.com

Gail Bird: Russian punch needles and supplies. www.GailBird.com

Henry Glass Fabrics: Some of the fabrics used in this book are from my fabric line "Sewing Room Social" for Henry Glass Fabrics. www.HenryGlassFabrics.com

The Gentle Art: Hand dyed embroidery floss. www.TheGentleArt.com

Introduction

But the fruit of the Spirit is love, joy, peace, patience, kindness, goodness, faithfulness, gentleness and self-control. Against such things there is no law.
Galatians 5:22-23

There was a time when the fruit of one's hands was a necessity—without cooking and sewing skills, a person and her family would be hungry and naked! Being industrious and hardworking were required for survival. Now, of course, in our modern, fast-paced society, we don't have to cook if we don't want to, and I know only one or two people who make their own clothes anymore. (Funny, just two generations removed from me, my grandmother made all of her own clothes!) We are fortunate that we can turn our creative urges toward making things that are no longer absolutely essential, but provide joy for us and others. In today's world, creativity is not required and many of us have lost our connection to our creative selves. We can walk into any retail shopping center and choose clothing and home goods that someone else designed and made, and food that someone else has prepared. Because of this hectic, sometimes robotic existence, I think a little bit of our soul has withered away.

Many of us, including me, find it satisfying to express our creativity through home décor projects or by making good food for family and friends. I find that nurturing my creative self, and using those gifts and skills for others, helps me to be more peaceful and kind, loving and patient. By connecting to the person that God made me to be, I am able to love others more easily. It took me a long time to figure that out. I spent years doing "practical" jobs because I thought that being an artist was frivolous or self-serving, and as a result my life was not nearly as fruitful as is could have been, because I was denying an essential part of who I am.

Like most people today, I find it hard to carve out time for creativity with so many other things beckoning for my attention. I have found that I must make creativity a discipline in my life, that I must be willing to let some dirty dishes sit in the sink and ignore my dusty furniture so that I can retreat to my studio to do that which makes me who I am. Creative ideas are often fleeting and must be allowed to flow while still fresh and alive. My family and I have learned to live in a house that is never completely clean (oh to have every room clean at the same time!) and to eat simple meals and the occasional take out. In exchange they get to live with someone who is much calmer and happier.

The projects here are quite varied—you will find projects for sewing machine stitching and hand stitching, and you may even want to try something new like decorative painting or punch needle embroidery! I never have less than 5 or 6 projects "under construction" at a time. Whatever I am in the mood to do, there is usually something waiting for me. There are always some things by the sewing machine to be sewn up, a painting project on the table ready for me to pick up my brushes, and at least two projects by the sofa for evening hand stitching. (And of course, while I am working, I am often thinking about what to make for dinner!) And speaking of cooking, I have included some favorite recipes. Some are old family favorites, and others are recent products of a spark of creativity in the kitchen. Cooking is another creative outlet for me. While I don't have time to cook and bake as much as I'd like, there are always tons of ideas for new culinary creations swimming around in my head.

I have tried to make my instructions as clear and thorough as possible. However, a book is not a substitute for an experienced instructor by your side to guide you. I highly recommend that you take advantage of every opportunity to take classes on new techniques or mediums. A good instructor can give you valuable tidbits of advice which will make your work much more efficient, enjoyable, and aesthetically pleasing.

Remember to have fun. That is what it is all about! Feel free to substitute colors, materials, or techniques to make each project uniquely you. For example, the Pineapple Welcome wall hanging could be done with darker colors and hand appliqué or even with wool for a more primitive look. This is about expressing your creativity and your style and enjoying the process.

A final note: always sign and date your work! I have been in museums with glorious quilts and handwork displayed. Sometimes the work has been signed, but too often it is resigned to anonymity due to the lack of a signature. Sadly, the creator was, and will forever remain, unknown. I often think that it never even crossed the minds of the women who made these works of art that some day their work might be displayed in a museum for thousands to admire. So please, label your quilt. Sign and date your work, and include any other information pertinent to the quilt. Future generations will thank you!

May your hands, and indeed, your life, be fruitful!

Jacquelynne

General Instructions

This is not an exhaustive handbook on the subject of quilting. It is simply the way I do things. There are many excellent books and online resources regarding the many how-tos of sewing and quilting.

SEWING AND QUILTING BASICS

Supplies

All of the fabrics I have used in my projects are 100% cotton. It is your choice whether or not to pre-wash your fabric. Pre-washing will remove sizing and excess dyes, and it will shrink your fabric slightly. However, many quilters prefer the body that new, unwashed cotton fabrics have. Also, when a quilt made with unwashed fabric is washed after completion it will pucker slightly, giving the quilt a vintage or antique look (obviously this is an advantage or a disadvantage, depending on the look you want). If you choose not to pre-wash your fabric, test dark and red dyes before using in your project to make sure they don't run.

For quilt backing I usually use standard width (about 42") cotton fabric instead of buying the extra wide fabric that is available. It takes more time to piece together, but usually I find that I have enough scraps leftover from my quilt top and in my stash to make a backing that is large enough. This saves money and makes a quilt back that is certainly more interesting. It's almost like having a reversible quilt!

As for batting, there are many types: cotton, wool, bamboo, polyester. The subject probably deserves an entire book of its own (or at least a few chapters). This is mostly a personal preference. I prefer a thin batting that gives the appearance of an old vintage quilt. The type of batting used also depends on how the quilt is intended to be used. Will it be used on a bed, as a wall hanging, or as a table topper? Does it need to be extra warm? How often will it be washed? Will it be hand quilted or machine quilted? These are just a few of the things to consider when choosing batting.

Cutting Your Fabric

Cut fabric across the width of the fabric unless otherwise noted (the width of the fabric runs perpendicular to the selvedge edges of the fabric). Some of my cutting directions will instruct you to cut a strip that is a certain measurement by the width of the fabric (wof) rather than a particular length. In most cases you will be instructed to trim off the selvedges after cutting your width of fabric strips. Your fabric will fit on your cutting table better and be easier to handle if it is folded in half lengthwise.

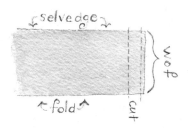

When making a project with similar fabrics (for example, more than one blue) it is best to label your fabrics before you cut, and then label the pieces as you cut (for example, blue #1). I simply write the fabric description on a scrap of paper and pin it to the fabric. You will avoid a lot of confusion and frustration if you label your fabric pieces. Everything will be easy to identify and piecing will be quicker.

Sewing and Pressing

Unless otherwise specified, sew all seams with right sides of fabric together, using a scant ¼" seam allowance. A scant seam allowance is just a thread shy of ¼". This will give you more accurate measurements as you sew blocks and rows together because it will make up for the loft of fabric that gets lost in the fold of the seam. You can mark the plate of your machine, and/or use a ¼" foot.

Practice and decide what works best for you. You may even find that a walking foot works well for piecing. (A walking foot feeds the top layer of fabric and bottom layer of fabric evenly through the machine.) I discovered this once when I was too lazy to change the foot on my machine and just left the walking foot on. I found that my piecing seemed to be more accurate with the walking foot than with my ¼" foot. Now I leave it on my machine most of the time.

Press your seams after each step. Traditionally, seams in a quilt are pressed to one side, toward the darker fabric. However, sometimes a seam just wants to go the way it wants to go! In this case, if the lighter fabric is not so light that the seam allowance will show through on the top of the quilt, go ahead and press toward the lighter fabric. The quilt police will probably not show up on your doorstep! Also, keep in mind that your blocks will lay flatter if the seams are pressed going in opposite directions, so that they lock together when placed next to each other.

All of that being said – more and more I have been pressing my seams open (the quilt police *might* end up on my doorstep for that statement!) I have found that it makes my blocks, and subsequently the entire quilt, lay flatter. Because I machine piece, I have confidence in the durability of my seams. However, there is some controversy over this. Visit some quilting forums on the Internet and see what I mean! But I think generally there is never just one right way to do things, and this is something you can experiment with and decide what works best for you.

A word about pinning

I pin *everything*, even when I am chain piecing. Taking the extra few minutes to pin will make your piecing more accurate. Sometimes, such as for triangles that seem to want to fishtail at the end of the seam, I place a tiny dot of basting glue just at the corners for extra security.

I usually piece borders diagonally (except for striped fabric when a straight seam makes it easier to match the stripes). To piece diagonally, remove the selvedges from your fabric strips. Place the strips right sides together at a 90 degree angle (I do this on my cutting mat and use the lines on the mat so that I get a perfect 90 degree angle). Use a ruler to mark a line from corner to corner, and then pin the pieces together. Sew on the line. Open up the seam to make sure that the strips are sewn evenly, and then trim away the excess fabric. Press the seam open to reduce bulk.

In a perfect world our actual quilt sizes would be exactly what they are mathematically calculated to be. But how often does that happen? Before cutting the borders to the lengths listed I recommend measuring your quilt across the *center of the quilt* to get an accurate border measurement and cut the borders accordingly.

Many of the projects call for topstitching. Topstitching usually runs parallel and next to a seam and may be done with thread that matches your fabric or with a contrasting color thread. Topstitching lies on the top of your fabric and is visible, so try to be as neat and accurate as possible. A walking foot is handy for flat, neat topstitching. If you have not topstitched before, simply gather up some scraps and practice, practice, practice. Your topstitching will look lovely in no time. (Hint: the better your thread matches your fabric, the less any mistakes will show.)

There will be times when you will be instructed to backstitch a seam. This provides durability to your seam. Backstitching is not required when piecing quilt blocks or sewing blocks or rows together. If the instructions do not specifically call for backstitching, then it is not necessary. To backstitch, simply make a few forward stitches in your seam, then go back 2 or 3 stitches, and then proceed forward with your seam.

Bias Tape for Vines

A couple of projects call for bias tape to make vine appliqués. Cutting strips on the bias (diagonal) rather than on the straight of the grain will make them bend and curve more easily.

To make the bias tape first cut bias strips. Fold the fabric in half diagonally. Then fold one corner toward the center, and then fold the other corner toward the center (your fabric will look kind of like an envelope).

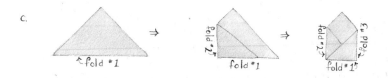

Use a rotary cutter to trim off folded edge #1. Cut strips to desired width (each cut will produce 2 strips).

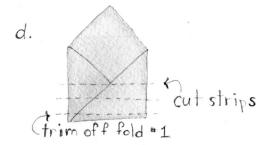

Piece the strips together diagonally (see diagram b at left).

Fold the strip in half lengthwise with WRONG sides together and press. Sew the folded strip along the raw edge using a ¼" seam allowance. Press the seam open so that it lies on the back of the bias strip. Trim seam allowance to about ⅛" so that it doesn't show on the front of the bias strip (There are also bias tape gadgets available to make this step faster and easier.)

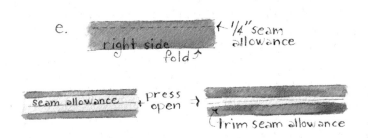

MACHINE APPLIQUÉ

My projects employ machine appliqué. While I love the look of hand appliqué and enjoy the process, I have found that I just don't have the time to complete all of the projects that I would like. Machine appliqué makes my projects go faster so I can move on to the next one! If you enjoy hand appliqué, all of the projects here can certainly be done that way. *All of the appliqué patterns in this book are reversed.* Most of the appliqué in this book, with the exception of the Citrus Peel Quilt and some of the larger appliqué pieces in the House on a Hill Quilt, use fusible machine appliqué. Fusible machine appliqué utilizes fusible webbing to adhere the appliqué pieces firmly to the background fabric before doing your machine stitching around the edges. Use lightweight fusible webbing when working with cotton quilting fabrics.

For fusible machine appliqué, photocopy the pattern sheet and use a light box or tape your pattern to a sunny window. Trace the patterns onto the paper side of the fusible webbing. If a pattern piece is labeled "reverse," flip the pattern page over and trace the wrong side of the pattern. Cut out fusible webbing pieces, leaving about ⅛" border around each piece. Iron pieces onto the WRONG side of the fabric, following the manufacturer's instructions. Cut out the pieces on the drawn lines. Place the fused fabric pieces RIGHT side up on your background fabric, removing the paper backing as you go. Some pattern pieces will have a dotted line to indicate where the pieces overlap. Using an up and down motion with your iron, fuse appliqué pieces to background fabric following manufacturer's instructions for temperature and steam/no steam. (Avoid sliding your iron back and forth over the pieces until they are completely fused, as this can move them out of position.)

Machine appliqué around the edges using desired stitch, such as zigzag, blanket stitch, blind hem, etc. I usually use a zigzag stitch that is fairly narrow, and a medium to long stitch length (for a zigzag, stitch length refers to how close together the stitches are). I don't care for the look of a tight zigzag (satin stitch). I prefer that my piece have a more handmade look, but that is my personal preference. Sometimes I use thread that matches the appliqué piece, and sometimes I use a contrasting color of thread. If you are new to machine appliqué, using a thread that matches your appliqué will hide any imperfections in your stitching. Do some practice stitching on scraps to get the look that you like, and to make sure your machine tension is correct.

I do not backstitch the beginning and ending of my machine appliqué stitching. Instead, when finished, I use a sewing needle to pull the top thread to the back of the fabric, then tie it off with the bobbin thread and trim the excess threads. This gives a nicer finish than having noticeable backstitching on the front of your appliqué piece.

If you choose not to use fusible webbing, trace the patterns onto the paper (dull) side of freezer paper. Cut out the freezer paper shapes on the drawn line. Iron to the WRONG side of the fabric, leaving about a ½" space around each shape. Cut out the fabric shapes, leaving ⅛ to ¼" around each shape (patterns do not include seam allowance unless noted). Press the edges under, toward the dull side of the freezer paper (if it is an edge that will be overlapped by another appliqué piece, you do not need to turn it under). Once the fabric has cooled, remove the freezer paper. Some people prefer to leave the freezer on the back of the piece while they appliqué it, but I prefer to not have to deal with removing it later. Use appliqué pins or basting glue to attach the appliqué pieces to the background fabric. Machine appliqué as described above, or hand appliqué. If the freezer paper has been left on the shapes, carefully make a small opening in the background fabric behind the appliqué, and remove the paper. If you are having trouble removing the paper, you can dampen it with water to soften it.

BINDING

After your quilt has been quilted (either by machine or by hand), trim away excess batting and backing fabric so that it is even with your quilt top. Cut binding strips that are 2 ½" wide by the width of the fabric. Trim off the selvedges and piece the strips together diagonally as shown in diagram b on page 6; press seams <u>open</u>. You will need enough binding to go around the edges of the quilt, plus about 10 extra inches. Fold one short edge of the binding under (toward the wrong side) ¼" and press. Fold the binding strip in half lengthwise RIGHT sides out and press. (See diagram f).

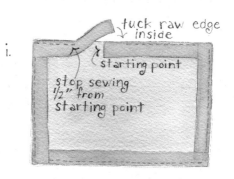

Fold binding to back side of quilt and hand stitch in place using matching thread. Blind stitch the miters at the corners.

Starting with the end of the binding that has been pressed under, place the binding on the top (RIGHT side) of the quilt (See diagram g), with the raw edges of the quilt and binding aligned (do not start at a corner). Pin in place.

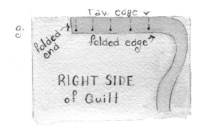

Sew the binding to the quilt, starting 1" from end of binding and using a ¼" seam allowance. Stop sewing when you get ¼" from the first corner and backstitch. Cut the threads and remove the quilt from the machine. Fold the unsewn binding strip up at a 90-degree angle to the sewn binding, then fold it back down on itself. (See diagram h.) Pin binding in place. Starting ¼" from the corner edge and backstitching, continue to sew the binding to the quilt until you get to the next corner. Repeat for each corner.

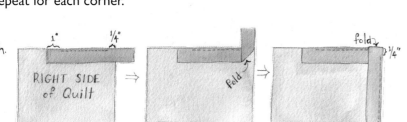

Stop sewing about ½" from your starting point and backstitch. Trim excess binding, leaving about ¾" to tuck inside starting edge of binding (see diagram i). Finish sewing binding to quilt. Hand stitch binding edges together using matching thread.

LABELING YOUR QUILT

Whenever you make a quilt – no matter the size – be sure to attach a label. Memories can fade, but the label will last as long as the quilt. I've included a couple designs for you to copy and use. You will find these and the instructions for attaching the label on page 63.

Satin Stitch
Make straight stitches across shape.

EMBROIDERY AND HAND STITCHING

For hand embroidery I trace my design onto the fabric with a washout fabric marker. There are a couple of different kinds of markers–some disappear automatically after a few days and some require water to be removed. I use the latter kind because often I work on my projects sporadically and need the design to remain on my project for longer periods of time. Use a marker with as fine a point or nib as you can find. When you are finished stitching a design, daub (do not rub) the fabric with a moistened cloth to remove the marker, then lightly press the design on the wrong side of the fabric so as not to flatten or distort the stitches.

To transfer the design, center your fabric right side up over the design and tape or pin it in place. Use a light box or sunny window to trace the design directly onto the fabric with the washout fabric marker. Place the fabric in an embroidery hoop or frame. I much prefer a plastic hoop to a wooden one, and I like to use a hoop that the entire embroidery design can fit into. However, sometimes this is not possible (for example, the embroidered border on the House on a Hill Quilt), in which case you can just move the hoop as necessary, but always remove the hoop when you are done stitching for the day. Leaving fabric in the hoop for too long will distort it.

When using hand dyed threads, which are not guaranteed to be colorfast, you may soak them in warm water first to remove any excess dye, and then lay the thread flat on a cloth to dry. Embroidery floss usually consists of six strands of thread. Cut a length about 15" long, and then pull out threads one at a time. For example, if the project instructions require 2 strands of floss, pull out a thread from the floss and lay it on the table or on your lap, then pull out another. Place the second thread next to the first, and then thread your needle. When working with variegated or hand dyed flosses, place the strands next to each other in the same direction, to keep the colors consistent.

Backstitch
Bring needle up through A. Go back & down through B & up through C. Go down through A & up through D. Continue.

Running/Gathering Stitch

French Knot
Bring needle up, wrap thread around needle 2-3 times. Bring needle down right next to the spot where it came up. Pull slowly & gently until knot forms on top of fabric.

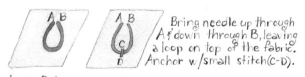

Bring needle up through A & down through B, leaving a loop on top of the fabric. Anchor w/small stitch(C-D).

Lazy Daisy
aka Detached Chain

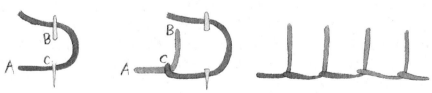

Blanketstitch
Bring needle up through A. Go down through B and up through C. Continue.

9

House on a Hill

QUILT

Finished size approximately 71" x 83"

I think we all have a personal meaning for the word "home". For some of us, we have one place that we feel is home–maybe it is the place we currently live, or the place where we grew up. Maybe it is a particular town, or a particular house or apartment, or even our favorite room. Some may have moved around quite a bit and thus carry their sense of home around in their heart, with no connection to a particular physical or geographical location. Whatever and wherever home is to you, it is most certainly a place to feel safe, secure and loved. It is the place where dreams sprout and grow. It is the place that gives us both our roots and our wings.

This quilt was done with machine appliqué. Remember, the more variety of fabrics you use, the scrappier your quilt will look. If you don't have the time or inclination to make a large quilt, the quilt center along with the embroidered border would make a great wall hanging, just leave off all the extra borders.

FABRIC AND SUPPLIES

- Cream: 1 ⅝ yards
- Purple (borders, appliqué): ⅝ yard
- Light Yellow Plaid (borders): ½ yard
- Green #1 (borders, vine appliqué): 1 ⅞ yard
- Green #2 Plaid (top hill appliqué): ½ yard
- Green #3 (bottom hill appliqué): ⅝ yard
- Green #4 Diamond Print (roof appliqué): ¼ yard
- Red (borders): ¾ yard
- Green/Blue Stripe (borders, appliqué): 1 yard
- Aqua Blue (binding, appliqué): 1 yard

- Additional fat quarters or scraps for appliqué and pieced borders:
  - 2 Yellow fat quarters
  - 1 or 2 additional Blues
  - 1 or 2 additional Greens
  - 1 or 2 additional Purples
  - 1 or 2 additional Reds
  - 1 or 2 additional Browns

- Backing Fabric of choice: 5 yards (40-42" wide)
- Batting of your choice

- Embroidery floss: 2 skeins Peacock blue (The Gentle Art #0910)
- Thread for machine appliqué: white or cream, yellow, green, blue, purple, red, brown

CUTTING INSTRUCTIONS
(cut fabrics in the following order)

CREAM
31" x 41" (quilt center appliqué background; will be trimmed to 30 ½" x 40 ½" after appliqué is completed)
1 - 5 ½" x 40 ½" strip (embroidered border #4)

PURPLE
9 - 1 ½" x wof strips (2 strips will be used for border #1, 7 strips will be used for border #8)

LIGHT YELLOW PLAID
2 - 4 ½" x 40 ½" strips (border #2, appliquéd vine background)

GREEN #1
4 - 6" x wof strips. Label these "side borders" (border #6)
4 - 6 ½" wide x wof strips. Label these "top & bottom borders" (border #6)
Cut enough 1 ½" wide bias strips to make a strip 112" in length for bias strip vines (see general instructions page 6).

RED
5 - 4" wide x wof strips (border #5)

GREEN/BLUE STRIPE
8 - 4" wide x wof strips (border #9)

Make the embroidered border (#4)
Fold border fabric in half to find center point and mark with a pin. Line up center point of fabric with center point on pattern. Use a light box or a sunny window to trace the pattern onto the fabric with a washout fabric marker. Embroider with the backstitch using 2 strands of blue embroidery floss. See embroidery instructions on page 9.

Make the appliquéd center
Fold green fabrics for hills in half, right sides together. Place patterns on fold as indicated and trace patterns for hills onto the back of the green fabrics. Cut out on the traced line. Trace the pattern for the sun onto the back of the yellow fabric (use one of your yellow fat quarters) and cut out on the traced line. Press under curved edges of green and yellow fabrics ⅛" as indicated on pattern.

Trace remaining pattern pieces (windows, roof, chimney, flowers, stems, leaves, dragonfly) onto the paper side of fusible webbing. Draw a 12" x 12" square on the fusible webbing for the house. Cut out and fuse to wrong sides of fabrics as explained in general instructions, page 7. Cut fabric pieces out on the traced line.

Referring to the diagram on page 64, arrange appliqué pieces on the background fabric. The straight edges of the sun align with the straight edges of the background fabric, and the straight edges of the green hills align with the straight edges of the background fabric. These edges will be sewn into the seam allowance. The window backgrounds are layered between the house and the window. The outer edges of the small flowers are about 2" from the side edges of the background fabric.

Carefully remove all pieces except the stems and leaves. Fuse stems and leaves to background; machine appliqué. Place the flowers back on the background; appliqué.

Place the house, roof and chimney on background and appliqué.

Place the dragonfly, door, windows and window backgrounds on the background fabric; appliqué. Make sure the window background is behind the window. When appliquéing the windows, use white or cream thread to match the window frames and appliqué around the outer and inner edges of window frames.

Securely pin or glue baste the sun and hills to the background fabric and machine appliqué folded edges only.

Trim background fabric (including attached edges of sun and hills) to 30 ½" x 40 ½". Remember, the raw straight edges on the sun and hill appliqués will be sewn into your seam allowance.

Make the vine and leaf appliquéd side borders (#2)

Sew bias strips together to make 2 strips each 56" long (this will give plenty of extra for you to play with). Make vines (see general instructions page 6). Referring to the photo, pin the vines to the Light Yellow Plaid borders. You will have several inches of bias left over. Machine or hand appliqué the vine in place, trim off the extra bias strips so that the edges are even with the short edges of the border (ends of vines will be included in the seam allowance).

Trace 10 border leaf patterns onto fusible webbing, cut out and fuse to the wrong side of the assorted green fabrics (I used 2 different green fabrics, you can use as many as you want, it just depends how scrappy you want your quilt to look). Six leaves will face the outer border, and the 4 reversed leaves will face the quilt center. Arrange the leaves on the border, fuse in place and machine appliqué.

Make the pieced top and bottom borders (#3)

Cut 20 rectangles from your assorted fat quarters and appliqué scraps, each 4 ½" x 3 ½". Sew 10 of them together along the 3 ½" sides into a strip. Sew the remaining 10 together into another strip.

Cut 2 of the Purple border strips (for border # 1) to 40 ½" long. Sew these strips to the sides of the appliquéd quilt center.

Sew the Light Yellow Plaid vine border (#2) to the other sides of the quilt center.

Sew the pieced borders (#3) to the top and bottom of the quilt.

Sew the embroidered border (#4) to the bottom of the quilt.

Make the red border (#5)

Make the corner blocks. Cut 2 - 4 ⅜" squares from Green #1 fabric and 2 - 4 ⅜" square from one of your yellow fabrics. Cut each square in half diagonally to make 4 green triangles and 4 yellow triangles (diagram a). Sew the green triangles to the yellow triangles along the long edge to make 4 squares, each 4".

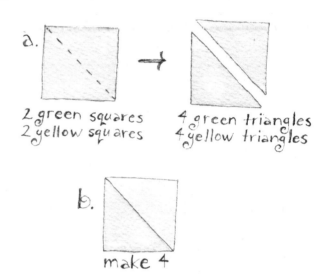

Sew 3 of the Red border strips together into one long strip, using a diagonal seam (see general instructions page 6). Cut the long strip into 2 strips, each 51 ½" long. Sew to the sides of quilt.

Cut 2 of the Red border strips to 40 ½" long. Sew a green/yellow square to each end with a yellow triangle adjacent to the red strip. Sew to the top and bottom of the quilt.

Make the green border (#6)

Piece the 4 side border strips (6" wide) together diagonally. From this long strip, cut 2 borders, each 58 ½" long. Sew to the sides of the quilt.

Piece the 4 top and bottom border strips (6 ½" wide) together diagonally. From this long strip, cut 2 borders, each 58 ½" long. Sew to the top and bottom of the quilt.

Make the pieced border (#7)

You will make the pieced borders out of assorted 2 ½" squares. There are two ways to do this. The first is to cut several strips from different fabrics, each 2 ½" wide. Sew 3 or 4 of them together along the long edges, and then cut these into 2 ½" Sections.

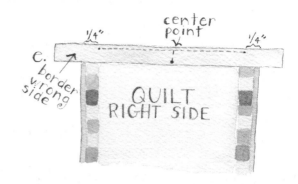

With the wrong side of the quilt facing you, cross one of the border ends over the other. Mark a 45-degree angle on the border strip.

Sew the groupings together until you get the correct number of squares in each border. You will need 2 strips with 35 squares each, and 2 strips with 31 squares each.

You can also use up your scraps and cut 130 assorted 2 ½" squares and sew them together to make the pieced borders.

Either way, sew the strips with 35 squares each to the sides of the quilt, and then sew the strips with 31 squares each to the top and bottom of the quilt.

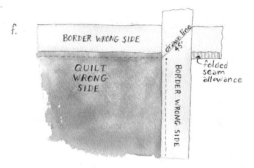

Fold the quilt diagonally, right sides together, so that the edges of the borders are aligned. Pin in place and sew along line, backstitching at the corner.

Make the purple border (#8)

Piece the remaining 7 purple strips together diagonally into one long strip. From this long strip, cut 2 strips, each 74 ½" long. Sew to the sides of the quilt.

Cut 2 strips, each 64 ½" long. Sew to the top and bottom of the quilt.

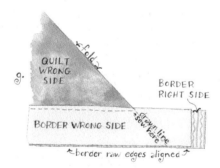

Check to make sure the border lies flat.

Make the striped border (#9)

Trim the selvedges from the 8 striped strips and piece together in pairs, so that you have 4 strips. When piecing striped borders together, I prefer to use a straight seam rather than a diagonal seam, as it is easier to match the stripes using a straight seam.

Mark the center point on all four sides of the quilt by folding it in half and placing a pin at the fold.

Fold the strips in half and mark the center point of each strip.

Place a strip on the quilt, right sides together, matching the center points. Starting at the center and working towards the ends of the quilt and border, pin the border to the quilt. The border strip will extend beyond the end of the quilt. Sew the border to quilt, starting and stopping ¼" from the end of the quilt and backstitching. Repeat on remaining 3 sides of quilt.

Trim away the excess border.

Repeat with the remaining 3 corners.

Quilt as desired.

Bind with blue fabric.

Creamy Dijon Chicken

This recipe was given to me by my mother-in-law. She has been making this recipe for about 30 years and it was a favorite dinner of my husband and his brother when they were growing up. Now I make it for our family and my kids love it too. It hasn't changed except that I added the Dijon mustard. You can also make this ahead—cover the chicken with cheese and the soup mixture; cover casserole and refrigerate. Make the stuffing mix and butter mixture and refrigerate separately, then sprinkle it over top when you are ready to bake it.

   4 boneless skinless chicken breasts halves
      (2 whole breasts, about 1 ½ - 2 lbs.)
   4 oz. Swiss cheese, sliced or shredded
   1 can condensed cream of chicken soup, undiluted
   ¼ c. white wine
   1 ½ T Dijon mustard
   ½ stick (4 T) butter
   1 ½ c. herb seasoned or chicken flavored stuffing mix
      (about one-half of a 6 oz. box)

Preheat oven to 350 degrees. Spray a 9" x 13" baking dish with nonstick spray.

Cut breast halves in half again. Arrange in baking dish. Top with cheese.

Combine soup, wine and mustard, stirring well. Pour sauce evenly over chicken.

Melt butter in a medium sized microwaveable bowl. Stir in stuffing mix to coat.

Sprinkle stuffing over chicken. Bake covered 40 minutes. Remove cover and bake another 10 - 15 minutes until chicken is done.

Serve with Outrageous Horseradish Cheddar Potatoes, page 48.

Pineapple Welcome

WALL HANGING

Approximate finished size 17" x 23".

Greet your guests with this welcoming wall hanging. In the 15th and 16th centuries, Spanish explorers learned that when Caribe natives placed a pineapple at the village entrance, the Spaniards were welcome there. During colonial times, because of its rarity, the pineapple represented a host's affluence, and it was the image of welcome and hospitality. Today, the pineapple remains a universal symbol of hospitality.

FABRIC REQUIREMENTS

- Black (background, borders, binding): ⅝ yard
- Yellow #1 (borders, appliqué): ⅜ yard
- Yellow #2 (pineapple, appliqué, pieced border): 1 fat quarter or scraps
- Light Lime Green (bottom "Welcome" border, appliqué, pieced side borders): 1 fat quarter
- Medium Green (top appliquéd border, appliqué): 1 fat quarter
- 2 different Oranges (appliqué and pieced side borders): scraps
- 2 or 3 different Greens (in addition to Light Lime Green and Medium Green listed above; appliqué and pieced side borders): scraps
- Backing fabric: ⅝ yard
- Lightweight cotton batting: 20" x 24" piece

ADDITIONAL MATERIALS

- Black embroidery floss
- Thread: green, yellow and orange for machine appliqué
- Fusible webbing
- Washout fabric marker

CUTTING INSTRUCTIONS
(cut fabrics in the following order)

BLACK

Cut background 9" x 12"
Cut 2 strips, each 18 ½" x 1 ½", for the side borders
Cut 2 strips, each 18" x 1 ½", for the top and bottom borders
Cut 4 rectangles, each 1 ½" x 2 ¼", for the outer borders

YELLOW #1

Cut 2 strips, each 18 ½" x 2 ¼", for the side borders
Cut 2 strips, each 12 ½" x 2 ¼", for the top and bottom borders
Cut 4 squares, each 2 ¼" x 2 ¼", for the border corners

LIGHT LIME GREEN

Cut 1 piece 13" x 5" for the "Welcome" border

MEDIUM GREEN

Cut 1 piece 13" x 4" for the top appliquéd border

ASSORTED YELLOWS, GREENS AND ORANGES

Cut 22 rectangles, each 1 ½" x 2 ½", for the pieced side borders

Appliqué

Trace appliqué patterns onto the paper side of the fusible webbing. Cut out, leaving about ⅛" around each piece. Fuse to wrong sides of fabrics (fabric colors indicated on pattern). Cut out on the traced line. See general instructions on page 7.

Referring to the diagram on page 77, arrange pineapple and leaves on black background, noting overlapped areas. When arranging your appliqué pieces, remember that the border piece will be trimmed to 8 ½" x 11 ½" after the appliqué is complete, and that you will need to include at least ¼" for seam allowance. So be careful not to arrange your appliqué pieces too close to the edge of the background. Fuse the pieces to the background and machine appliqué using a zigzag stitch (or other desired stitch) and matching thread.

Arrange circles on pineapple; fuse and machine appliqué. Trim black background to 8 ½" x 11 ½", centering the pineapple and leaving at least ½" from the outside edge of the appliqué to the edge of the background. Remember to leave ¼" seam allowance all around the background piece.

Arrange the large circles on the medium green border piece (again remembering that the background will be trimmed when the appliqué is complete). From left to right, the order of the circles is A, B, C, D. Fuse and machine appliqué. Trim to 12 ½" x 3 ½".

Embroidery

For bottom border, center and trace "Welcome" onto the right side of the 13" x 5" Light Lime Green border piece. Place in an embroidery hoop and backstitch with 4 strands of black embroidery floss. Remove marker lines (see general instructions page 9). Lightly press from the wrong side of the fabric. Trim to 12 ½" x 4 ½".

Assemble the Wall Hanging

PIECED BORDER

Sew 11 of the 1 ½" x 2 ½" rectangles (assorted colors) together, along the longer edges, so you have a strip that is 11 ½" x 2 ½". Repeat with remaining 11 pieces. Sew the pieced borders to the sides of the pineapple appliqué piece.

Sew the appliquéd Medium Green border to the top of the wall hanging.

Sew the "Welcome" border to the bottom of the wall hanging.

OUTER BORDER

Sew an 18 ½" x 1 ½" Black strip to the sides of the wall hanging.

Sew an 18 ½" x 2 ¼" Yellow #1 strip to the sides of the wall hanging.

Sew the 18" x 1 ½" Black strips to the top and bottom of the wall hanging.

Sew a black 1 ½" x 2 ¼" rectangle to each end of the 12 ½" x 2 ¼" Yellow #1 strips. Sew a 2 ¼" Yellow #1 square to the ends of each of these strips. Sew completed strips to the top and bottom of the wall hanging.

Quilt and bind.

Hanging Sleeve

To add a hanging sleeve, cut a piece of fabric that is 2 ½" x 16". Fold the short ends under ¼" toward the wrong side of the fabric and machine stitch in place. Fold the long ends under ¼" and press. Pin sleeve to back of wall hanging, about 1" from the top edge. Hand stitch the long edges of the sleeve to the back of the wall hanging. Place a wooden dowel through the sleeve and attach string or ribbon for hanging.

Pineapple Bread Pudding

If you come to any holiday gathering at our house you will most likely find this dish on the table. It is incredibly easy and goes especially well with ham, so we serve it every year at Easter dinner. It is my brother's favorite, and he actually gets angry with me when I don't make it–so we usually have it on Thanksgiving and Christmas, too! I know it looks like a dessert, but it's my opinion that something sweet on your dinner plate isn't a bad thing (would it be too audacious to count this as a fruit serving?)

This is one of those recipes that many families have their own version. This one came from a friend of my mother's about 25 years ago, and we've been making it ever since.

    ½ cup butter
    1 cup sugar
    4 eggs
    ½ teaspoon vanilla
    20 oz. can crushed pineapple, drained
    5 or 6 slices of bread, cubed
       (about 4 cups)

Preheat oven to 350 degrees. Cream butter and sugar; add eggs and beat well. Add vanilla and pineapple. Gently fold in bread until combined. Place in a buttered 2-quart casserole and bake uncovered for 1 hour.

OH SUNNY DAY!

TEA TOWEL

I find that a walking foot makes topstitching the ribbon and edges of the towel much easier. If you don't have a walking foot, just take your time and feed the fabric through your machine slowly to get a nice straight, even stitch. For a really quick and easy project, use a kitchen towel purchased from the store. Follow the instructions for appliqué and eliminate the ruffle.

FABRIC AND SUPPLIES

- Green striped linen or lightweight twill: ¾ yard
- Green solid linen or twill (for back of towel): ¾ yard
- Orange cotton fabric for ruffle: ⅛ yard
- Green ¼" wide grosgrain ribbon: 1 ¼ yard
- Scraps of light, medium, and dark yellow cotton fabric for appliqué
- Embroidery floss: White and Dark Yellow (DMC # 728)
- Yellow thread for machine appliqué
- Green thread to match ribbon and linen or twill fabric for machine topstitching
- Orange thread to match ruffle for topstitching
- Fusible webbing for machine appliqué

Instructions

Cut the green striped linen to 26 ½" x 18 ½". Repeat with green solid linen. Trace the lemon appliqué designs onto the paper side of fusible webbing. Iron to wrong side of cotton fabrics according to manufacturer's instructions. Remove paper backing and place, adhesive side down, on one end of the green striped linen, layering the light yellow pieces under the dark yellow (rind) pieces (see diagram a for placement). Iron in place according to manufacturer's instructions.

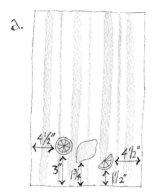

Use a zigzag stitch with yellow thread to machine appliqué.

Embroider the details

Use 3 strands of white embroidery floss to back stitch the segment lines. Use 3 strands of dark yellow embroidery floss and a detached chain stitch for the seeds.

Cut 2 pieces of ribbon each 19" long. Place one piece about 1" from the raw edge of the green striped linen (below the appliqués) and pin in place. Note that the cut edges of the ribbon will extend about ¼" beyond the edge of the linen. Place the other piece of ribbon about 5" from the first piece of ribbon (above the appliqués) and pin in place. See diagram b for placement.

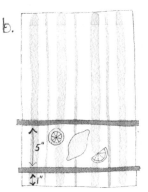

Use green thread to topstitch the ribbon in place, about 1/16" from the edges of the ribbon. Trim ribbon ends so that they are even with the edges of the linen.

Make the ruffle

Cut a piece of orange fabric 3" x 36". Fold the short ends under ¼" toward the wrong side of fabric; press. (See diagram c.)

Fold strip of fabric in half lengthwise with right sides out; press. (See diagram d.)

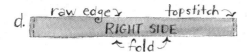

Use orange thread to machine topstitch the short ends together, or slipstitch ends together by hand. Cut a piece of thread about 24" long, and use it to make a running stitch about ¼" from the raw edges (stitch length should be about ¼"). Pull thread to gather the ruffle until it is 18" long. Tie off the thread.

Place green striped linen on table right side up. Pin the raw edge of the ruffle to the bottom edge of the linen (linen will extend beyond ruffle end about ¼"). Machine stitch in place, about ⅛" from edge. (See diagram e.)

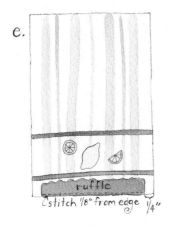

Pin unstitched corners of ruffle back to prevent them from getting sewn into the next seam. (See diagram f.)

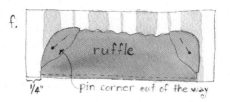

Place the green striped linen and the solid linen pieces right sides together and pin. Sew together, using a backstitch or locking stitch at beginning and end of seam, and leaving an opening about 6" long for turning. (See diagram g.)

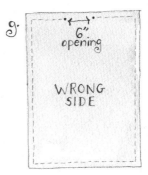

Turn towel right side out; push the corners out. Press the edges of the towel. Pin opening together. Topstitch around towel, ¼" from edge, using green thread.

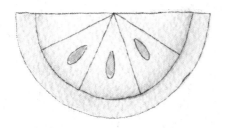

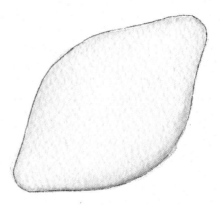

Sunshine Chicken Soup

A light, bright soup with a lovely lemony color–perfect for a spring luncheon or as an appetizer. This has become a "new classic" in our family–everyone loves it.

2 large bone-in chicken breasts (about 2 ½ lbs.)
1 medium onion, cut into eighths
4-6 cloves of garlic, peeled
½ lb. carrots, peeled and cut into 1" chunks
2 stalks celery, cut into 1" chunks
12 cups (3 quarts) cold water
1 T salt
½ cup freshly squeezed lemon juice (juice of about 2 lemons)
2 eggs
1 or 2 ripe avocados

Place all ingredients except lemon juice, eggs and avocado in a large stock pot. Bring to boil, then reduce heat and simmer, covered, for about 45 minutes until the chicken is done and the vegetables are tender.

Remove the chicken from the pot and allow it to cool. Place the broth from the pot in the refrigerator for about 1 hour.

Remove the chicken from the bones, discarding the skin. Shred the chicken and set aside.

Skim fat from the broth. Place half of the broth and vegetables in a blender or food processor and puree. Repeat with the remaining broth and vegetables. Return the pureed broth and vegetables to the stock pot and simmer, uncovered, for about 1 hour.

In a large bowl, whisk together lemon juice and eggs. Very slowly, so that eggs do not curdle, whisk in 2 cups of hot broth. Add the lemon juice, egg and broth mixture to the stock pot. Stir in the shredded chicken.

Slice the avocados. Ladle soup into bowls and garnish with avocado.

Chocolate Peanut Butter Cupcakes

Makes 24 cupcakes.

Boxed cake mix makes these cupcakes a cinch to make. My family's favorite part of making these is "testing" the Hershey's Kisses as they unwrap them.

18.25 oz. box Devil's Food Cake Mix
Ingredients listed on cake mix box to prepare batter

Peanut Butter Filling
⅔ c. confectioner's sugar (10X)
¼ tsp. vanilla
½ c. creamy peanut butter
1 ½ T. butter, softened

Buttercream Frosting
3 c. confectioner's sugar
7 T. butter, softened
1 tsp. vanilla
3 T. half and half

Topping
⅓ c. chopped salted dry roasted peanuts
24 Hershey Kisses, unwrapped

Preheat oven to 350 degrees. Line 24 muffin cups with paper liners.

Make peanut butter filling: Mix ingredients with mixer until well combined. Form into 24 balls, about ½ tablespoon each, and place on wax paper covered baking sheet. Set aside.

Make the cupcakes: Prepare batter according to box directions. Fill each muffin cup slightly more than half full. Place a peanut butter ball in the center of each cupcake and push down gently (it's OK if the batter does not completely cover the peanut butter.) Bake 15 minutes, until tops of cupcakes are just set. Allow to cool in muffin pans for about 1 minute, then carefully remove and place on wire rack to cool.

Make the frosting: Beat butter, sugar and vanilla until combined. Add half-and-half and beat until light and fluffy.

Frost cooled cupcakes. Top each cupcake with a Hershey's Kiss. Sprinkle with chopped peanuts and lightly press pieces into the frosting.

27

Cherished Recipes

BINDER

I can't think of a nicer bridal shower gift than a handmade recipe binder or a hand painted recipe box (found on page 56), full of favorite recipes from family and friends. Make copies of the recipe pages or recipe cards and include them with the shower invitations, so attendees can fill them out and bring their favorite recipe for the bride-to-be to the shower. If you have time, you could also make the Sweet Stuff Apron (found on page 23). Now that is a gift any new bride would surely cherish!

FABRIC AND SUPPLIES

- Aqua Blue fabric: ⅜ yard
- Floral fabric: ¼ yard
- Red fabric: 3" x 8" scrap
- Brown ric rac, ⅝" wide: 38" long (1 ⅛ yards)
- Thread for topstitching: brown, blue
- Standard Binder from office supply store: 1 ½" wide
- Small sharp scissors, such as manicure scissors
- Heavy duty fusible webbing (I chose not to appliqué around the word "Recipes" on the cover and just relied on the fusible webbing to hold it in place.)

Instructions

Cut the aqua blue fabric to 9" x 38". Cut the floral fabric to 4 ½" x 38". Sew them together along the long edges and press the seam allowance toward blue fabric.

Pin the ric rac over the seam and stitch with brown thread. Make one line of stitches right down the center of the ric rac.

Fold the short ends of the fabric cover under (towards wrong side of fabric) ¼" and press. Fold under again ¼" and press. Topstitch the folded edges with blue thread, a scant ¼" from the folded edge.

Place the fabric on work surface, right side up. Center the open binder on the fabric with the inside facing up. Fold one end of the fabric toward the binder so that it folds over the binder cover; pin in place. Remove the binder and sew the top and bottom of the folded end, using a ¼" seam allowance and backstitch at the beginning and end of the seam.

Clip the corners and turn the fabric cover right side out. Gently push the corners out and press. This will be the front flap of the binder cover.

Fold the long raw edges ¼" toward the wrong side of the fabric and press. Topstitch entire length of long edges with blue thread, ⅛" from folded edge.

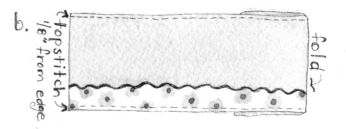

Trace the "Recipes" pattern onto the paper side of the heavy-duty fusible webbing. Cut out , leaving about ¼" outside the drawn line. Fuse to <u>wrong</u> side of the red fabric, according to manufacturer's instructions. Use manicure scissors to cut out the small areas (for example, the insides of the "e" and "s"). Cut out the remainder of the appliqué on the drawn line. Carefully remove the paper backing.

Place the front of the binder cover inside the front flap of the fabric cover. Arrange the "Recipes" appliqué on the front cover and pin in place. Remove the binder from the fabric cover and place the fabric cover on an ironing board. Fuse the appliqué in place, carefully removing the pins as you press. Remember to lift and press–do not slide the iron along the appliqué.

Place the binder back into the front flap of the fabric cover. Fold the fabric cover over back cover of binder so that it fits snugly; pin in place. Hand stitch fabric cover flap edges using matching thread.

Recipe Cards and Pages

You can either use a color copier to copy the recipe cards and recipe pages, or you can scan them into a program like Photoshop and print them (this would make it easier, especially for the recipe page, to get the design centered on the printed page.)

Recipe Cards

For the recipe card, color copy or print onto white cardstock. Cut out the card. Fold in half on the line indicated. If you run out of room on the front for writing your recipe, you can flip it over and use the back, too.

Recipe Pages

For the recipe pages, color copy or print onto an 8 ½ x 11" sheet of paper. You will find the colors will "pop" more if you use a coated paper, such as brochure paper. Punch holes along the left edge of each page and place in the binder.

Recipe:

from the kitchen of:

fold

RECIPE:

from the kitchen of:

RECIPE: _____

from the kitchen of: _____

Citrus Peel

QUILT

Approximate finished size 45" x 54"

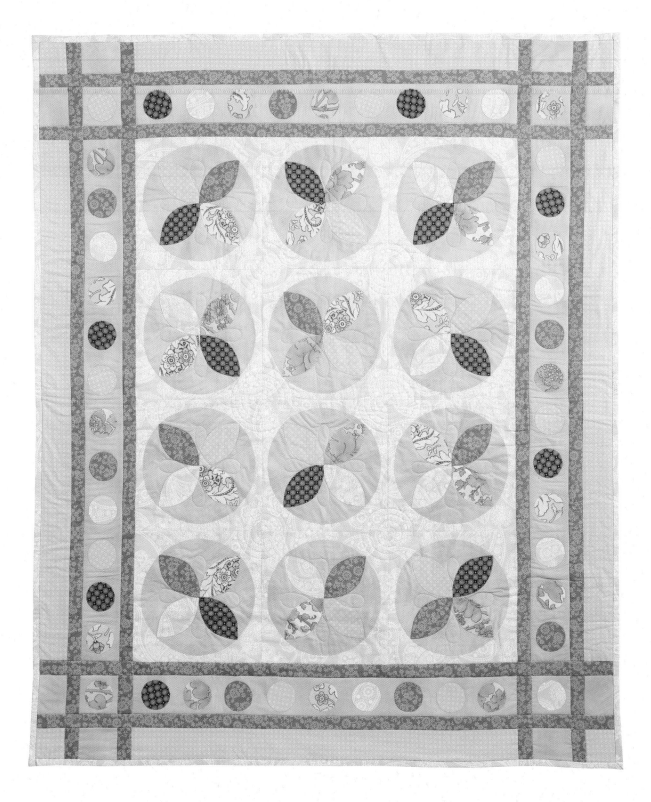

This is a takeoff on the classic orange peel block. The colors are so refreshing and remind me of a citrus salad–oranges, lemons and limes. The blocks are appliquéd so there is no need for curved piecing (I hear a sigh of relief from a few of you!). I prepared the circles and "peels" as I would for hand appliqué by turning the edges under and then machine appliquéd them. Of course, you could also hand appliqué the quilt. Unless you plan to use this quilt as a wall hanging, I don't suggest fusible machine appliqué for the project, as it will end up too stiff and bulky instead of comfy and snuggly.

FABRICS AND SUPPLIES

All fabric measurements are based on 40-42" width of fabric (wof)

 A. Orange small floral print: 1 yard (small borders, "peel" appliqués, small circle appliqués)
 B. Lime Green small print or tone-on-tone: ¾ yard (outer borders, "peel" appliqués, small circle appliqués)
 C. Light Green medium scale print or tone-on-tone: 1 ⅞ yards (block backgrounds, "peel" appliqués, small circle appliqués, binding)
 D. Gold solid: 1 ¾ yards (large circles, border for small circle appliqués)
 E. Gold medium to large-scale print/floral: ⅜ yard ("peel" appliqués, small circle appliqués)
 F. Orange and brown small graphic print/dots: ⅜ yard ("peel" appliqués, small circle appliqués)
 G. Yellow and Green medium scale print/floral: ⅜ yard ("peel" appliqués, small circle appliqués)
 • Backing Fabric: 3 ½ yards
 • Batting of your choice
 • Matching threads for machine appliqué: yellow, green, orange, gold

CUTTING INSTRUCTIONS FOR BORDERS AND BLOCKS

ORANGE:
Cut 10 - 1 ½" x wof strips for borders

LIME GREEN:
Cut 4 - 3" x wof strips for outer borders

LIGHT GREEN:
Cut 12 - 11" x 11" squares (these will be trimmed to 10 ½" after appliqué is completed)

GOLD SOLID:
Cut 4 - 3 ½" x wof strips for small circle appliqué borders
Cut 4 - 3 ½" squares for border corners

Preparing the Appliqués

Trace and cut out 46 small circles and 48 peels from freezer paper. Arrange pieces shiny side down about ½" apart, on wrong side of assorted fabrics: A, B, C, E, F, and G. Iron freezer paper to fabrics. Cut out, leaving ⅛" to ¼" seam allowance around each shape (pattern pieces do not include seam allowance). Turn under edges for appliqué.

Cut out 12 large circles from freezer paper. Arrange pieces shiny side down about ½" apart on wrong side of Gold solid (fabric D). Iron freezer paper to fabric. Cut out, leaving ⅛" x ¼" seam allowance around each shape. Turn under edges for appliqué.

Making the appliqué blocks and assembling the quilt center

Fold each Light Green square in half diagonally and press lightly, then fold in half diagonally again and press. Open up squares. Place a large Gold circle in the middle of each square and appliqué using matching thread.

Arrange 4 assorted "peels" on each large Gold circle, lining up the points of the peels with the fold marks in the squares. Appliqué using matching thread. See diagram a.

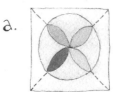

Lightly press blocks from back to remove fold lines.

Trim blocks to 10 ½" each, centering the appliqué.

Sew blocks together into 4 rows of 3 blocks each. Sew rows together to complete quilt center.

Making the appliqué borders

Measure across the center of your quilt. It should measure 40 ½" x 30 ½." Adjust your borders accordingly.

Cut 2 of the Gold solid borders (3 ½" wide) to 30 ½." Arrange 9 small circles on each strip (leave at least ½" on each end to allow for a ¼" seam allowance).

Cut the remaining 2 Gold solid borders to 40 ½". Arrange 12 small circles on each strip, again leaving at least ½" on each end.

Place the 4 remaining small circles on the 4 Gold 3 ½" squares.

Appliqué small circles using matching thread.

The side borders

Cut 4 of the Orange (fabric A) 1 ½" border strips to 40 ½" long. Sew 2 of the strips to either side of the quilt.

Sew the 2 Gold borders (40 ½" long with 12 circles) to the orange border strips on either side of the quilt

Sew the remaining 2 Orange borders to the gold borders to either side of the quilt.

Cut 2 of the Lime Green (fabric B) 3" strips to 40 ½" long. Sew these strips to the sides of the quilt. Your quilt should now look like this:

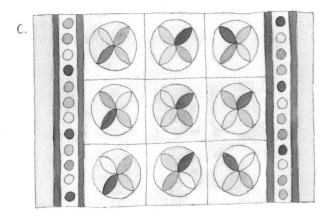

The top and bottom borders

Measure across the width of the quilt center. It should measure 45 ½." Adjust your borders accordingly.

Piece the remaining six Orange (fabric A) border strips into one long strip. Sub cut into 4 borders, each 45 ½" long. Save the scraps for the next step.

Sub cut the 1 ½" wide Orange strip scraps into 8 rectangles 3 ½" long and 8 rectangles 3" long.

From the Gold solid, cut 8 rectangles 3 ½" x 3".

Cut the two remaining Lime Green (Fabric B) 3" strips to 30 ½" long.

Sub cut the rest of the Lime Green 3" strips into 4 - 3" squares.

Assemble borders as follows

To either end of each Gold appliquéd border, sew a 1 ½" x 3 ½" Orange strip.

To either end of the borders, sew an appliquéd 3 ½" Gold square.

To either end of the borders, sew the remaining 1 ½" x 3 ½" Orange strips, then sew a Gold rectangle (3 ½" x 3") to either end.

make 2 borders like this:

To either end of the Lime Green 3" x 30 ½" strips sew an Orange 1 ½" x 3" rectangle. To these, sew the 3 ½" x 3" Gold rectangles. Sew a remaining Orange 1 ½" x 3" rectangle to either end, and then sew a 3" Lime Green square to each end.

make 2 borders like this:

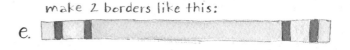

To each long side of the Gold appliquéd and pieced borders sew an Orange 1 ½" x 45 ½" border. Sew a Lime Green pieced border to the Gold/Orange border on each border unit.

make 2 borders like this:

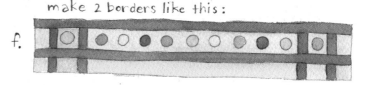

Sew borders to top and bottom of quilt.

Quilt and bind.

Orange Chocolate Chip Scones

Our family loves scones, and this is one of our favorite flavors. Drop scones like these are easy to make – they will become a favorite of your family, too. They are especially good right out of the oven when they are still warm and the chocolate is gooey. You can serve them plain, or with a little butter, jam, or marmalade (or for real authenticity serve with Devonshire or clotted cream, available at tea shops.) To get orange zest, grate the orange peel with a box grater. Take just the orange part–the white part is bitter.

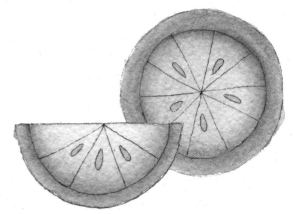

¾ cup whole milk
1 large egg
5 T sugar
2 tsp. orange extract
2 ¼ cups cake flour
1 cup old-fashioned rolled oats
1 T baking powder
½ tsp. baking soda
¾ tsp. salt
Zest from 1 medium orange (about 2 T)
¾ stick (6 T) cold butter
1 cup semi-sweet chocolate chips

Preheat oven to 400 degrees. Line a large cookie sheet with parchment paper.

In medium bowl, stir milk, egg, sugar and orange extract with a fork until well blended.

In a large bowl, stir together flour, oats, baking powder, baking soda, salt and zest. Use a pastry blender or 2 knives to cut butter into dry ingredients until mixture resembles coarse meal. Stir in chocolate chips.

Add the milk mixture to the dry mixture and stir just until blended. Do not over mix.

Drop onto cookie sheet at least 1" apart. Bake 11-14 minutes until edges are golden brown. Remove to wire rack to cool.

Makes 1 dozen scones.

Pear Make-Do

PINCUSHION

make-do (meyk'doo) *n. something that serves as a substitute, esp. of an inferior or prudent nature. Origin 1890-95.*
v. to manage with less than one would like by repairing or re-using old things instead of buying new ones.

A make-do is created from scraps and bits, and items that might otherwise be cast off. It is basically a stuffed item, in this case a pear, on some sort of base, often of a primitive or whimsical style. Use it as a pincushion or simply as an interesting conversation piece in your décor. I have included several words on the pattern page for you to choose from for your hanging tag, or you could write your own message on the tag. My tag says "patience" – a daily reminder for me to work on that characteristic of which I always seem to be in short supply!

FABRIC AND SUPPLIES

- Scraps of 3 different green fabrics
- Scraps of light and dark green wool
- Wool scraps, or wood or paper shreds
- Embroidery floss: brown (The Gentle Art Sarsaparilla #7015)
- Flower Pot approximately 4 ½" tall
- Styrofoam block
- Piece of lightweight cardboard
- Dark green or brown acrylic paint, paintbrush
- Poly-Fil
- Twig or stick
- Twine
- Beige and brown cardstock and paper scraps
- Fine point brown marking pen
- ⅛" hole punch
- Miscellaneous: pinking shears, decorative scissors, white glue, glue stick

Instructions

Trace the pear pattern (page 84) onto the wrong side of 3 different green fabrics. Trace or transfer the dots onto fabric. Cut the pieces out on the solid line.

Place 2 fabric pieces right sides together and pin. Sew together on the stitching lines between the dots, backstitching at the beginning and end of the seam. Sew the third fabric piece to one of the previous pieces, right sides together. Sew the unsewn edges together, right sides together, leaving an opening for turning (see pattern piece), and backstitching at the beginning and end of seams.

Turn pear right side out. There should be a small hole at the top and the bottom where the twigs will be inserted. Stuff the pear <u>firmly</u> with poly-fil. Hand stitch the opening closed. The poly-fil may be redistributed and evened out by gently squeezing and smoothing the pear from the outside.

To make the leaf, trace the large leaf pattern onto the dark green wool, and the small leaf onto the light green wool. Cut out. Use pinking shears to trim around the edges of the small leaf. Place the small leaf on the large leaf. Stitch leaves together by embroidering the veins, using a backstitch and 2 strands of brown embroidery floss, as indicated on the pattern piece (see general instructions on page 9).

Turn the flowerpot over and trace the top of the pot onto the piece of cardboard. Cut out about ⅛" inside of traced circle. Cut a circle in the middle of the cardboard that the stick can fit through.

Cut the Styrofoam block to fit snugly inside the flowerpot. Place the Styrofoam in the pot so that the top of the foam block is just below the top of the pot.

Place the cardboard circle on top of the Styrofoam; it should fit just inside the top of the flowerpot. Trim as necessary to make it fit. Remove the cardboard circle and paint it with dark green or brown acrylic paint. Allow it to dry, then put it back in the flowerpot and glue it down.

Break or cut a stick about 7 ½" tall. Place it through the hole in the cardboard and into Styrofoam block. Secure with glue. Push the pear onto the stick though the small hole in the bottom of the pear. Glue to secure.

Place a small twig in the hole at the top of the pear and secure with a small amount of glue. Use a small dot of glue to secure the leaf to the top of the pear.

To cover the top of the flowerpot, you may use shredded wool, paper or wood. If using wool, cut wool scraps into shreds that are about ⅛" wide. Cover the top of the Styrofoam with glue and cover with shreds.

Use a brown marking pen to trace the desired word onto beige paper or cardstock. Cut out around the word with pinking shears or decorative scissors. Trace the tag pattern onto brown cardstock and cut out. Use a glue stick to glue word label onto the brown tag. Punch a hanging hole in the corner of the tag with a hole punch.

Tie a piece of twine around the flowerpot. Secure with a small dot of glue if desired. Tie the tag onto the stick or twig with the twine.

Spiced Pear Upside-Down Cake with Ginger Cream Sauce

A twist on the traditional Pineapple Upside-Down Cake (also a family favorite). The Ginger Cream Sauce for this is divine. You will want to pour it on *everything*.

Cake
2 cups all purpose flour
1 tsp. ground ginger
1 tsp. ground cinnamon
½ tsp. ground nutmeg
1 tsp. baking soda
¾ tsp. salt
¼ cup molasses
½ cup light corn syrup
½ cup packed brown sugar
1 stick butter, melted and cooled
2 large eggs
1 tsp. vanilla extract
¾ cup milk

Pear Topping
1 stick butter, divided
⅔ cup brown sugar
2-3 large ripe firm pears, such as Bosc or Anjou (about ½ pound each)
18-20 whole cloves

Ginger Cream Sauce
1 cup sugar
1 tsp. ground ginger
2 sticks butter
1 cup half and half

Preheat oven to 350 degrees.

To make the pear topping, place ½ stick of butter in each of two 8" or 9" square cake pans. Place pans in hot oven until the butter melts and just starts to turn brown (about 5 minutes). Be careful not to burn the butter. Remove pans from oven. Add ⅓ cup brown sugar to each pan and stir until a paste is formed. Spread evenly over the bottom of the pans.

Carefully remove the core from the pears. If you do not have a corer, cut the pears first, then remove the core. Cut pears crosswise into ¼" slices. Arrange pear slices on bottom of pans; place a clove in the center of each pear slice.

In a large bowl, sift the flour, ginger, cinnamon, nutmeg, baking soda and salt. In another bowl whisk together the molasses, corn syrup, brown sugar, melted butter, eggs, vanilla and milk until well blended. Pour wet ingredients into the dry ingredients and stir until well blended. Pour batter evenly over pears. Bake until the center is set, about 30 minutes. Remove from oven and allow to cool 10 –15 minutes. Invert cakes onto serving plates (do not allow cake to cool for too long or they will not release from the pans.)

To make the sauce, stir together the sugar and ginger. Place in a medium sauce pan with butter and half and half. Carefully bring the mixture to a slow boil over medium heat, stirring constantly. Reduce heat to low and simmer for 10 minutes, stirring occasionally. Pour into a sauce or gravy boat and allow to cool until slightly warm or room temperature. Pour over individual servings of the cake and enjoy.

Fayette County Fair

TABLE RUNNER & PLACE MAT SET

Approximate finished sizes:
Table runner 13" x 45 ½"
Place mats 14" x 18 ½"
Napkins 10" square

The mix of plaid and floral with a liberal dose of red says country fair to me. This table set is an invitation to picnic right in your dining room whenever you'd like, no matter the weather (and no ants!). If you can't find a plaid that you like, a check or gingham would also work nicely for this design.

FABRIC AND SUPPLIES (to make 1 runner, 4 placemats and 4 napkins)

- Small Blue Floral Print: 2 yards
- Diagonal Red/Gray Plaid: 1 ¼ yards
- Red solid or tone-on-tone: 2 yards
- Gray solid: ⅝ yard
- Thread for appliqué and topstitching: gray, blue, and red
- Fusible Webbing
- Freezer paper
- Marking pen such as a Pigma Micron

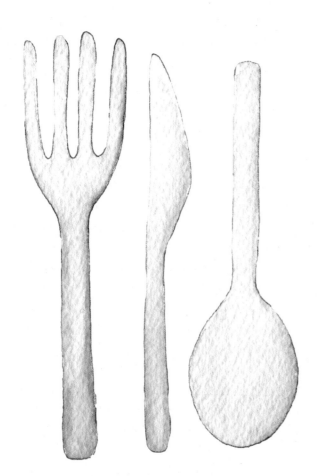

CUTTING INSTRUCTIONS

For the table runner
BLUE
1 - 10 ½" x 40 ½" rectangle for top

RED
1 - 13 ½" x 43 ½" piece cut parallel to selvedge for the back
2 - 2" x 40 ½" strips cut parallel to selvedge for the long borders
2 - 2" x 13 ½" strips for the short borders

PLAID
1 - 5 ¼" x wof for the curved edging

For 4 Placemats
PLAID
4 - 11 ½" x 14 ½" for the tops

BLUE
8 - 2" x 11 ½" strips for the short borders
8 - 2" x 17 ½" strips for the long borders
4 - 14 ½" x 17 ½" pieces for the backing

RED
1 - 15" x wof; trim off selvedges. Sub cut into 8 strips, each approximately 5" wide x 15" long

a.

selvedge (trim off)
cut
cut
cut
}5" each
cut
cut
cut
cut
15"
selvedge

For 4 Napkins
BLUE
8 - 1 ½" x 8 ½" strips
8 - 1 ½" x 10 ½" strips

GRAY
8 - 1 ½" x 8 ½" strips
8 - 1 ½" x 10 ½" strips

RED
4 - 8 ½" squares

PLAID
4 - 8 ½" squares

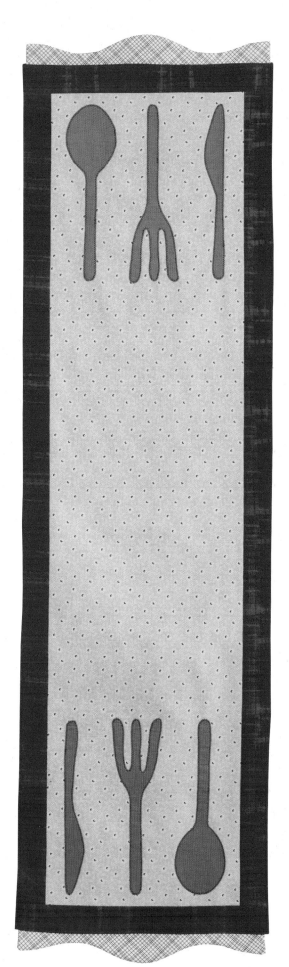

Making the table runner

Sew long (2" x 40 ½") red borders to blue table runner top. Sew short (2" x 13 ½") red borders to ends of table runner.

Place table runner top and red backing (13 ½" x 43 ½") right sides together and pin. Sew together along long sides (do not sew short sides). Turn right side out and press. (I found that the easiest way to press this is to first press the seams open, and then place wrong sides of fabrics together and press folded seam flat.)

Fold short (raw) ends of table runner in toward each other ¼" (toward inside of fabric) and press.

Trace appliqué patterns onto fusible webbing. Cut out and arrange on table runner top. Pin around appliqués to secure layers. Machine appliqué with gray thread.

To make curved edging, trim selvedges from plaid strip. Fold strip lengthwise, right sides together, and press. Trace the edging pattern onto freezer paper and cut out on the traced line. Iron freezer paper pattern to wrong side of strip, leaving at least ¼" around all sides. Trace around pattern with marking pen. Remove freezer paper pattern and repeat at other end of folded fabric strip. Pin fabric strip to hold layers together.

Sew the short straight ends and the curved side on the traced lines. When sewing curves, frequently lift the presser foot while leaving the needle down in the fabric, slightly pivot the fabric, then lower presser foot to continue sewing. Stitch slowly for best accuracy!

b.
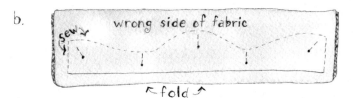

Cut out edgings. Leave about ⅛" seam allowance around the sewn lines, but cut directly on the long straight drawn (unsewn) line.

c.
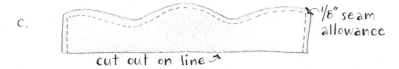

Turn edgings right side out using a point turner to **gently** push out the corners. Press.

Insert raw edge of edging into sides of table runner, position and pin in place.

Use red thread to topstitch around table runner, ⅛" from edge.

d.
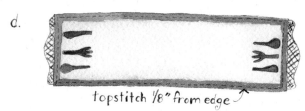

Making the place mats

Making the napkins

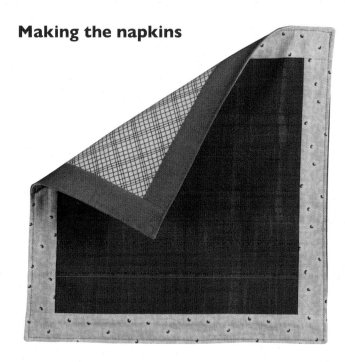

For <u>each</u> place mat:
Sew a 2" x 11 ½" blue border to each short side of the plaid place mat tops, then sew a 2" x 17 ½" blue border to each long side of the plaid place mat tops.

Lay the place mat tops and blue place mat backing (14 ½" x 17 ½") right sides together and pin. Sew together along the long sides only (do not sew short sides). Turn right side out and press. (See table runner directions for pressing tips.)

Fold short (raw) ends of place mats in toward each other ¼" (toward inside of place mats) and press.

Trace appliqué patterns onto fusible webbing. Cut out and arrange on place mat tops. Pin around appliqués to secure layers. Machine appliqué with gray thread.

To make the curved edging fold the 5" x 15" red strips lengthwise, right sides together, and press. Trace the edging pattern onto freezer paper and cut out on the traced line. Iron freezer paper pattern to strip, leaving at least ¼" around all sides. Trace around pattern with marking pen. Remove freezer paper pattern and repeat with remaining 7 folded fabric strips. Pin fabric strip to hold layers together.

Sew the short straight side and curved seams directly on the traced lines. Cut out as described in the Table Runner instructions (see diagrams b and c).

Turn right side out, gently push the corners out and press.

Insert raw edge of edging into sides of place mats; position and pin in place.

Use blue thread to topstitch around place mats, ⅛" from edge.

Sew the 8 ½" long borders to either side of each napkin (blue borders on red napkins; gray borders on plaid napkins.)

Sew 10 ½" long borders to remaining sides. Press.

Place a plaid napkin and a red napkin right sides facing. Sew together, using a ¼" seam allowance, and leave a 6" opening along one side for turning. Backstitch at the beginning and end of the seam.

Clip corners and trim seam allowance to ⅛" near corners.

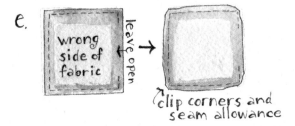

Turn right side out and press, turning edges of opening ¼" in toward each other. Pin opening closed.

Topstitch ⅛" from edge around all sides. Use blue thread on top and gray thread in bobbin and sew with the red and blue side facing up.

Repeat with remaining napkins.

BLT Macaroni & Cheese Cups

This is just fun – miniature macaroni and cheese with bacon, lettuce & tomato! It can be served as a side dish or an appetizer. For a side dish serve hot; as an appetizer it may be served hot or at room temperature. Also, the baked macaroni and cheese cups (without garnish) can be frozen. Take out as many as you need from the freezer and bake on a greased cookie sheet at 350 degrees for about 30 minutes, then garnish.

    16 oz. elbow macaroni
    12 oz. bacon, cooked and crumbled; drain grease, reserving 1 T in pan
    2 medium onions, chopped
    1 T butter
    1 tsp. garlic powder
    16 oz. part skim ricotta cheese
    8 oz. sharp cheddar cheese, shredded
    ½ cup milk
    ¾ cup sour cream
    ¾ cup shredded lettuce
    ½ cup finely chopped tomato

Preheat oven to 350 degrees.

Cook elbow macaroni in salted water about 9 minutes or until al dente (slightly firm). While macaroni is cooking, brown onions in skillet with reserved bacon fat.

Drain macaroni and return to pot. Add butter, bacon, onions, garlic powder, ricotta cheese and cheddar cheese; stir. Stir in milk. Add salt and pepper to taste.

Spray muffin tins with nonstick spray. Spoon macaroni mixture into tins, use a metal spoon to pack macaroni down (cups should be ¾ full).

Bake for 35 minutes, or until the edges are golden and bubbly (do not over bake). Remove from oven and use a knife to loosen around the edges. Leave macaroni in tins for 15 minutes to cool.

Carefully remove macaroni from tins onto a plate with a fork (if they are falling apart, let them cool a little longer). Top each with about a teaspoon of sour cream, sprinkle with lettuce and tomato.

Makes about 30.

Walk Around The Block

Finished size approximately 49" square

This is the perfect size to use as a table topper, or throw it on the back of a chair or sofa that needs a little pizzazz. Or, try sewing one up with pastels or brights for a baby or toddler quilt. For some reason, it reminds me of a little town, a place where I'd love to leisurely stroll and admire the cottages and gardens.

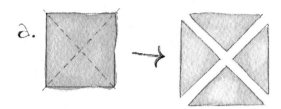

FABRIC REQUIREMENTS

- Light Green: ½ yard
- Floral on Ivory background: ¼ yard
- Blue: ¼ yard
- Red: 1 ⅜ yard
- Brown: ½ yard
- Light Beige: 1 ⅛ yards
- Stripe: 1 ½ yards
- Backing fabric: 3 yards
- Batting of your choice

CUTTING INSTRUCTIONS
(cut in the following order)

Border #2
LIGHT GREEN
Cut 4 - 1 ½" x wof strips

Border #3
RED
Cut 5 - 3 ½" x wof strips

Border #4
LIGHT BEIGE
Cut 5 - 3" x wof strips

Blocks
LIGHT GREEN
Cut 50 squares, each 2 ½" x 2 ½"

RED
Cut 50 squares, each 2 ½" x 2 ½"

LIGHT BEIGE
Cut 100 squares, each 2 ½" x 2 ½". Cut 13 squares, each 3 ¼" x 3 ¼", then cut diagonally into 4 triangles (total of 52 triangles). (See diagram a.)

BROWN
Cut 13 squares, each 3 ¼" x 3 ¼", then cut diagonally into 4 triangles (total of 52 triangles). (See diagram a.)

Block Border (Border #1)
BLUE
Cut 11 blocks, each 3 ½" square

FLORAL
Cut 11 blocks, each 3 ½" square

BROWN
Cut 22 blocks, each 3 ½" square

Assemble the Blocks

To make the "bow tie" block for the center of each larger block, sew each Light Beige triangle to a Brown triangle along a short side. You will have 52 triangle units. Sew these units together in pairs. This will yield 26 "bow tie" blocks, each 2 ½" (you will only need 25 of these for the quilt). See diagram b.

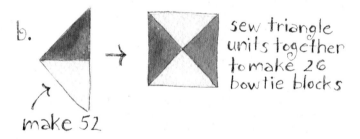

sew triangle units together to make 26 bowtie blocks

make 52

Sew 12 of the Brown and Light Beige bow tie blocks to a 2 ½" Light Beige square, along the <u>brown edge</u> of the bow tie block. Sew the remaining 13 bow tie blocks to 13 of the 2 ½" Light Beige squares, along the <u>Light Beige</u> side of the bow tie block. See diagram c.

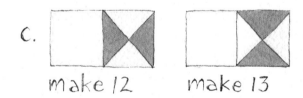

c.   make 12   make 13

Sew each of these units to the remaining 2 ½" Light Beige squares. You will have 25 units, each 6 ½" x 2 ½". See diagram d.

d.   make 12   make 13

Take each of the 2 ½" Red squares and sew to a 2 ½" Light Beige square to make 50 units. Onto the Light Beige block of each of these units, sew a 2 ½" Light Green square. This will yield 50 units, each 6 ½" x 2 ½". See diagram e.

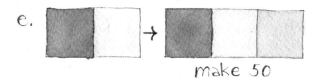

make 50

Sew a Red, Light Beige and Light Green unit to a Brown and Light Beige bow tie unit. Repeat with remaining 24 Brown and Light Beige units. See diagram f.

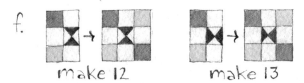

make 12   make 13

Sew the remaining Red and Light Green units to the Brown and Light Beige units so that the Red squares are in opposite corners to complete the blocks. You will have 25 blocks, each 6 ½" square. See diagram f.

Referring to photo on page 44, arrange blocks into 5 rows of 5 blocks each, alternating the vertical and horizontal Brown bow ties.

Sew the blocks together into rows, then sew the rows together to create the quilt center.

Assemble the Block Border (Border #1)

Referring to diagram g, sew 10 blocks together, alternating the Blue, Floral, and Brown 3 ½" squares. Repeat with 10 more blocks to make 2 rows. Referring to diagram, sew to sides of quilt.

2 rows of 10 blocks - sew to sides

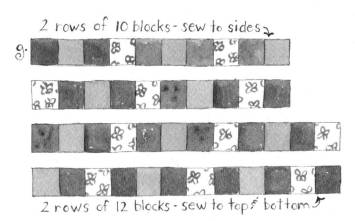

2 rows of 12 blocks - sew to top & bottom

Sew 12 blocks together and repeat with remaining 12 blocks, to make 2 rows. Sew to top and bottom of quilt.

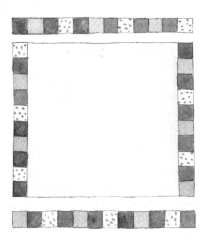

Add the Remaining Borders

Cut 2 of the Light Green border #2 strips to 36 ½" each and sew to the sides of the quilt.

Cut remaining 2 Light Green border #2 strips to 38 ½" each and sew to the top and bottom of the quilt.

Cut 2 of the Red border #3 strips to 38 ½" each and sew to the top and bottom of the quilt.

Sew the remaining 3 border strips together to form one long strip as described on page 6 of the general instructions. From the long strip, cut 2 strips, each 44 ½" long. Sew one strip to each side of the quilt.

Sew the Light Beige border #4 strips together as described in the general instructions. Cut 2 strips each 44 ½" long and sew to sides of quilt. Cut 2 strips, each 49 ½" long and sew to the top and bottom of the quilt.

From the striped fabric, cut bias strips 1 ½" wide and make about 216" of bias tape for the vine border.

Pin bias tape vine to Light Beige border #4, referring to the photo on page 44. For the corners, I folded the bias tape to make an angle instead of a curve—you may simply curve the bias tape in the corners if you prefer. Hand or machine appliqué the vine to the border. Hint: *Your bias tape will be a little longer than necessary, I recommend not trimming this excess until you are almost finished appliquéing the vine to the quilt.*

When you have only a couple of inches of vine left to appliqué, trim off the excess bias tape, leaving enough to turn under. See diagram h.

Quilt and bind with red fabric.

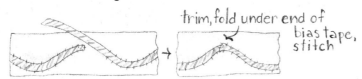

h.

trim, fold under end of bias tape, stitch

Outrageous Horseradish Cheddar Potatoes

You won't find this on The American Heart Association's list of approved recipes! This is definitely something I make on special occasions. It is so delicious and rich, you may feel the need to take a walk around the block (or maybe just take a nap) after indulging.

The horseradish adds a nice little "kick." Keep in mind that horseradish loses its potency after it has been open in the refrigerator for a while, so you may need to adjust the amount accordingly, and to your individual taste. If you don't like horseradish, you can leave it out and add a little crushed garlic instead.

    3 pounds Yukon Gold or other waxy potato, peeled
        and cut in half
    ¾ stick (6 T) butter
    ½ pint light cream or half and half
    8 oz. sharp cheddar cheese, shredded
    2 T prepared horseradish
    Salt and freshly cracked pepper to taste

Preheat oven to 350 degrees. Spray a 3 qt. casserole with nonstick spray.

Cook potatoes in salted water until just fork tender (slightly underdone). Drain and return to pot.

Over low heat, add butter to potatoes and mash with hand masher; potatoes should be slightly chunky.

Stir in the remaining ingredients.

Spoon into a casserole dish. Bake covered 1 hour until edges are golden and center is hot.

Cheery Cherry
PUNCHNEEDLE PILLOW

Many of us who "collect hobbies" have punchneedle tools in our sewing box. I love the unique look of punchneedle embroidery done with hand dyed threads. If you don't have a punchneedle tool, you could use a backstitch to embroider the cherry design as a stitchery. And if you haven't given punchneedle a try yet, ask your favorite quilt or needlework shop if they offer classes – it is fun, quite simple, and really addictive! You may just find that it's another good hobby to add to your "collection."

FABRIC AND SUPPLIES

- Weaver's cloth or muslin for punchneedle background, 12" square (Weaver's cloth is the commonly recommended fabric for punchneedle embroidery, but I have found that tightly woven muslin also works)
- Ivory cotton fabric, 12 ½" x 6 ½"
- Scraps of fabrics in green, red, blue
- Brown fabric: 2 strips, each 1 ½" x 12 ½"
- Striped fabric for ruffle: 2 strips, each 4" x 24"
- Fabric for back of pillow, 12 ½" square
- Piece of ric rac, ribbon, or other trim: 12 ½" long by ⅜" to ½" wide
- Sewing thread to match above ric rac or ribbon
- Embroidery threads from The Gentle Art:
  - Evergreen #0150 (1 skein)
  - Celery #0170 (3 skeins)
  - Cherry Wine #0330 (3 skeins)
  - Maple Syrup #0440 (1 skein)
  - Blue Spruce #0140 (2 skeins)
  - Butternut Squash #7020 (1 skein)
- Poly-fil
- 8" x 11" punchneedle frame or 10" plastic embroidery hoop
- 3 strand punchneedle tool
- Pigma Micron 01 pen

INSTRUCTIONS

Using a light box or sunny window, trace pattern onto center of Weaver's cloth or muslin with a Pigma pen. Place fabric onto frame or in embroidery hoop, making sure it is as taut as possible and that the grain of the fabric has not become distorted. You may have to re-tighten the fabric occasionally as you work the design. Using 3 strands of embroidery floss, work the pattern according to the colors shown on the pattern sheet. See page 9 in general instructions regarding the use of hand dyed/variegated threads.

Remove fabric from frame or hoop. Trim away excess fabric, leaving about ¼" of fabric around the punchneedle design. Turn under the fabric edges and hand applique the punchneedle design to the center of the ivory fabric rectangle. (See diagram a).

Cut 12 squares, each 2 ½", from assorted scraps. Sew the squares into two rows of 6 squares each. Sew the rows together. Sew the rows to the bottom of the punchneedle rectangle.

Pin the ric rac or ribbon over the seam that joins the scrappy rows with the punchneedle rectangle. Using matching thread, topstitch the trim to the fabric. If using ric rac, sew one line of stitches down the center. If using ribbon or other straight trim, sew a line of stitches down each edge.

Sew brown fabric strips to top and bottom of pillow front.

To make ruffles, press short ends of striped fabric strips under ¼" toward wrong side. Fold strip in half lengthwise with right sides out. Hand stitch or machine top stitch the short sides closed. Fold strip in half to find center point and mark center point with a pin or washout marker. (See diagram b).

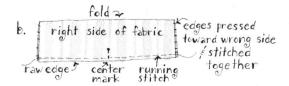

Make a running stitch, with ¼" long stitches, about ⅛" from the long raw edges of the strips.

Fold pillow top in half to find center point on each side and mark with pin.

Place ruffle strips on the right side of the pillow top, raw edges aligned and center point marks aligned. Pin each end of the ruffle ¼" from end of pillow top, and pin together at center where marked. Pull thread to gather fabric strip. Distribute gathers evenly along edge of pillow top and pin securely. Sew ruffle to pillow top ⅛" from edge. (See diagram c).

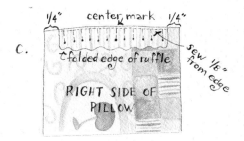

Place pillow top and pillow backing right sides together and pin. You can pin the edge of the ruffle out of the way so it doesn't get caught in your seam. Sew together using a ¼" seam allowance, backstitching at the beginning and ending of your seam. Leave a 4" opening at the bottom for turning.

Turn pillow right side out. Stuff with Poly-fil. Hand stitch opening closed.

a.

weaver's cloth → ¼" seam allowance → applique design on ivory fabric | turned under edge

Cherry Cheese Tart
with Almond Oatmeal Crumble

Toasting the almonds, or any other nut, makes a huge difference in the taste-simply place them in a dry non-stick frying pan over medium heat, stirring occasionally, until they are fragrant and golden. You have to watch them carefully, as they will burn quickly if left unattended. Cool and use in your favorite recipe.

Crumble Topping

⅛ tsp. salt
¼ cup flour
¼ cup old fashioned oats
⅓ cup sugar
¾ cup sliced or slivered almonds, toasted
¼ tsp. ginger
1 tsp. cinnamon
4 T butter, slightly softened

Cheese Filling

8 oz. cream cheese
⅓ cup sugar
1 tsp. vanilla

21 oz. can of cherry pie filling
17.3 oz. box of puff pastry

Remove pastry from box and thaw according to package instructions. While waiting for pastry to thaw, make the topping.

To make the topping, stir all dry ingredients together in a large bowl. Use a pastry blender or 2 knives to cut in butter. Cut into coarse meal. Refrigerate for one hour.

Preheat oven to 400 degrees.

To make the filling, beat together cream cheese, sugar, and vanilla until light and fluffy.

Unfold puff pastry and place side by side on large parchment paper covered baking sheet. (If both sheets do not fit on your baking sheet, just use 2 separate baking sheets). Bake the pastry until it starts to puff but is not yet golden (about 10 minutes). Remove pastry from oven.

Spread puff pastry with the cream cheese mixture (pastry will "deflate"). Top with cherry pie filling. Sprinkle with crumble topping mixture.

Return to oven. Bake 15 minutes until pastry is golden brown and center looks set.

Heartfelt Home

FLOOR MAT

Wool is one of my favorite materials to work with—no edges to turn under! I chose to do the decorative stitches in embroidery floss so that they would stand out, and then I did my appliqué with matching cotton thread so that most of my stitches would not show. If you prefer all of your stitches to show, then feel free to use embroidery thread or wool thread for both the appliqué and the decorative stitches.

I created this as a floor mat design because wool is quite durable. But if you can't bear to walk on it, feel free to use it as table topper or wall hanging.

Every house where love abides
And friendship is a guest,
Is surely home, and home sweet home
For there the heart can rest.
~Henry Van Dyke

FABRIC AND SUPPLIES

- Wool (preferably hand-dyed) in the following colors:
  - Black: 24" x 30"
  - Terra Cotta: 10" x 15" for flower pot
  - Green: ⅛ yard or scraps for flower pot base, leaves, flower centers
  - Teal: ⅛ yard for stems, letters, bird wing
  - Yellow: ⅛ yard or scraps for stripes on flowerpot and flowers
  - Assorted scraps: dark pink solid, dark pink plaid, light pink plaid, lavender, light blue, dark blue plaid, medium blue for flowers, hearts and bird
- Embroidery floss from The Gentle Art:
  - Poppy (pink) #0760,
  - Peacock (blue) #0910,
  - Spring Grass (green) #0180
- Cotton thread to match wool colors for appliqué
- Green cotton fabric for binding: 1 yard
- Backing fabric: cotton, 3⁄4 yard
- Freezer paper, small plate, chalk pencil, fabric basting glue, pins

INSTRUCTIONS

Trace pattern pieces onto paper side of freezer paper, leaving about ¼" between each piece. Cut out about ⅛" outside the line. Using a warm iron, fuse the shiny side of the freezer paper pieces to wool as indicated on pattern piece. Cut out on line. Carefully remove freezer paper from wool.

Referring to the pattern pieces and photo on page 90, do decorative stitching on bird wing, bird's eyes, and veins on leaves.

Use Poppy (pink) embroidery thread to blanket stitch the dark pink plaid heart to the light pink plaid flower center.

Use yellow cotton thread to appliqué the bird's beak to the head.

Use matching cotton thread to appliqué the flower centers to the flowers, using small stitches (See diagram a).

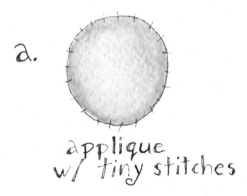

a.

applique w/ tiny stitches

Place a dinner plate on a corner of the black wool and use a chalk pencil to trace a curved edge onto the wool. Repeat with remaining corners. Cut the rounded corners on the drawn line.

Cut the teal and yellow strips. This can be done with scissors, but you will get a nicer, straighter edge with a rotary cutter. Cut strips ¼" x about 18". Cut 4 strips from teal wool, and cut 2 strips from yellow wool.

Pin a yellow strip across the top of the flower pot in a wavy line. Pin a yellow strip across the bottom of the flower pot in a line that curves up toward the edges. (You will have excess wool at the ends of your strips. This will be trimmed off later.)

Referring to the pattern pieces on pages 88 and 89 and photo, use teal strips to write the H, m, and e in "Home". For the loops in the "H" and "m" fold the wool strip back upon itself (this is OK because wool usually doesn't have a wrong or right side. Also, this will require a lot of pins to hold in place). Use the blue plaid heart as your "o".

When you are happy with the layout of the stripes and lettering, trim off excess yellow strip. Glue stripes, letters, and heart in place by carefully removing just a pin or two at a time and placing a small spot of fabric basting glue to hold, then replace pin to hold the piece in place until glue is dry.

Blanket stitch around the heart with Peacock (blue) embroidery thread. Use matching cotton thread to appliqué the stripes and the rest of the letters to the flowerpot.

Referring to the photo below, arrange all of the pieces on the black background. Use remaining teal strips for stems. Stems will tuck under the flowers and flowerpot. The Green flowerpot base will tuck under the flower pot. When happy with the placement, use pins or fabric basting glue to hold the pieces in place. Appliqué pieces to black background using matching cotton thread.

Place backing fabric on table, wrong side up. Place wool, right side up, on top of backing fabric. Trace around the wool onto the backing fabric. Cut the backing fabric out about ⅛" inside the drawn line. Place backing fabric and wool wrong sides together and pin.

To bind the floor mat, cut 2 ½" bias strips from green fabric and sew together end to end, referring to the general instructions on page 5. You will need about 107" of bias strip. Fold strip in half lengthwise, right sides out, and press.

Pin raw edge of bias strip (binding) to the edge of the wool mat. At the corners, do not pull the strip too tight; allow a slight gather of the bias strip on the folded edge. When you come back to your starting point, leave excess strip (it will be trimmed away later). See diagram b.

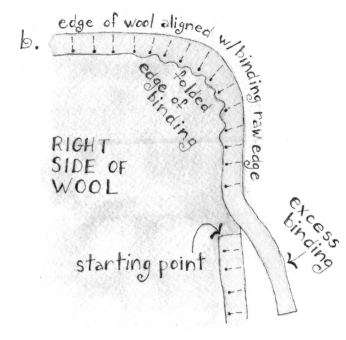

Machine stitch binding to floor mat, using a ¼" seam allowance, and stopping about 1" from your starting point. Remove pins and make sure you are happy with the way your binding folds to the back of the floor mat, especially at the corners.

Trim excess bias strip, leaving about ½". Turn the end of the binding under about ¼" so it overlaps starting point (see diagram c). Machine stitch remainder of binding.

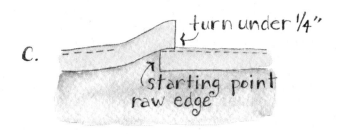

Turn folded edge of binding toward back of floor mat; hand stitch in place.

Rustic Sausage Casserole

I use fresh herbs for this. The recipe calls for rosemary and thyme, but really you can substitute any combination of fresh herbs you like; oregano and sage would also be good. If you don't have fresh herbs, use dry but cut the amount by half. To save myself a little time, I buy a bag of peeled baby carrots and cut them in half. Although this is technically a casserole, I serve it in deep bowls, like a stew, with crusty bread for soaking up the broth.

   1 pound mild or sweet Italian sausage (either bulk or links that have been
      removed from the casing)
   1 pound boneless, skinless chicken thighs, cut into 1" pieces
   1 pound carrots, peeled and cut into 1" chunks (about 3 cups)
   3 medium onions, cut into 1" chunks (about 3 cups)
   6 cloves garlic, peeled and cut in half
   1 ½ pounds Yukon Gold potatoes (about 4 medium), scrubbed and cut into
   1" chunks
   1-28 oz. can of diced tomatoes, including liquid
   1 cup white wine
   2 T fresh rosemary, chopped
   1 T fresh thyme, chopped
   1-15 oz. can of cannellini (white) beans, rinsed and drained

Preheat oven to 350 degrees.

In a large deep skillet, brown the sausage and break up with a wooden spoon. Remove to a bowl or plate.

Add chicken in a single layer to hot skillet, and do not stir until chicken is well browned. When browned, stir and continue to brown. Remove to bowl or plate.

Add onion, garlic and carrots to the skillet and cook over medium to medium high heat until vegetables start to brown (but do not burn). Sprinkle with salt and pepper. Add sausage and chicken back to the skillet.

Add potatoes, tomatoes, wine and herbs to the skillet and cook for about 10 minutes until bubbling.

Stir in the beans.

Transfer to two large casseroles, dividing liquid evenly between the casseroles. Bake covered for 1 hour.

Field Fresh

RECIPE BOX

Recipes

SUPPLIES

- Wooden Recipe Box: 4" tall x 5 ¾" wide x 6 ¼" deep
- Delta Ceramcoat Acrylic Paint:
  - Black Green
  - Sea Grass
  - Leaf Green
  - Chamomile
  - Butter Yellow
  - Tompte Red
  - Black Cherry
  - Palomino Tan
- DecoArt Americana Acrylic Paint: Light Avocado
- Delta Ceramcoat Matte Interior Varnish
- Palette: paper, plastic or glass (you can use a coated paper plate or plastic plate, or an old china plate)
- Paint brushes: 1" flat, #2 flat, #6 flat, #0 round, #1 round, 3⁄8" slanted shader
- Loew Cornell White Transfer Paper
- Stylus or pen, masking or painter's tape, water basin, paper towels

Instructions

Reduce or enlarge the pattern on page 92 as necessary to fit your box. You can also transfer the pattern onto a wooden plaque, or a flower pot, or trace it onto an apron or table cloth and paint it with fabric paints.

Practice blending your paint and making dots on your palette before working on your box. Always use nice fresh paint. If the paint on your palette starts to dry out and get "gunky" just squirt out some fresh paint on a clean spot on your palette. Don't worry about shading your fruit perfectly–a rustic or primitive painted look on this project is nice. If you don't love your shading, wait for the paint to dry completely and then go in and add a little more. Don't try to paint over paint that is still damp; it will pull up and make the paint uneven. If you are perpetually impatient (like yours truly) you can dry the paint with a hair dryer in between coats to make things go faster.

If you make a mistake while painting either wipe it away with a damp paper towel while the paint is still wet, or wait for it to dry and paint over it. I always have several paper towels handy while painting for wiping away mistakes or spilled paint, etc. If you are right handed work left to right, and if you are left handed work right to left to avoid paint smears.

Find matching recipe cards on page 30.

Measure border 1 ¼" from top and bottom of lid and draw a light pencil line across the box.

Paint top and bottom borders of lid and lid sides using Chamomile paint and a 1" flat brush.

Paint center part of top of lid and box bottom using Black Green paint and a 1" flat brush.

Tape pattern to top of box and place a piece of transfer paper under the pattern. Trace onto box using the stylus or pen. Tape apple pattern to side of box and trace; repeat with other sides of box.

When painting the design, go just over the white line to cover it.

Use a #6 flat brush to paint watermelon slice and center apples with Tompte Red (this is a rather transparent color and will require a few coats. Be sure to allow the paint to dry between coats. Paint over where the seeds will be. You can re-trace the pattern later or just freehand paint them).

Use a #2 flat brush to paint strawberries and cherries with Tompte Red.

Use a #1 round brush to paint the inner watermelon rind with Chamomile. Use a #2 flat to paint the middle

watermelon rind with Sea Grass. Use a #1 round brush to paint the outer watermelon rind with Leaf Green.

Paint pear and green apples using Sea Grass and a #6 flat brush. Wet a ⅜" slanted shader brush and blot lightly on paper towel. Dip pointed end only into Leaf Green, brush lightly across palette to blend color across brush. There should be paint on the pointed edge graduating to water only on the other edge. (See diagram a.) Paint along edges of pear and apples to shade. Allow paint to dry. Repeat until pear and apples are shaded as desired, allowing paint to dry in between layers of color.

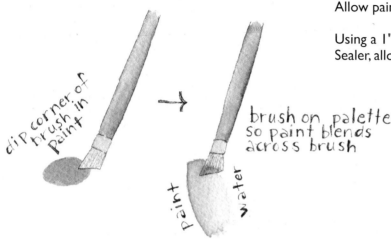

Use shader brush to shade watermelon, cherries and strawberry with Black Cherry.

Use a #1 round brush to paint the pear leaf and strawberry leaves with Light Avocado. Paint the cherry leaf with Leaf Green.

Use a #0 round brush to paint stems on the cherry, pear, apples and strawberry with Palomino Tan. Paint veins on pear, cherry and strawberry leaves with Sea Grass. Paint seeds on watermelon and strawberry with Black Green.

Use a #1 round brush to paint the apple leaves with Light Avocado. Use a #0 round brush and Sea Grass to paint veins on the apple leaves.

Use a #1 round brush and Sea Grass to paint "Recipes" on the lid of the box.

Use masking or painters tape to tape off the edges of box lid. Use a #2 flat brush and Leaf Green paint to paint a checkered pattern in border. Allow to dry well. Remove tape.

Tape off checkered border and center portion of box top. Use a #2 flat brush to paint stripe with Tompte Red (this will take several coats). Allow to dry and remove tape.

Dip the end of a paint brush handle into the Butter Yellow paint, and using a quick, steady motion, tap the end of the handle onto one of the Leaf Green squares. Repeat with each square, wiping the handle off and dipping it into paint for each dot.

Freehand draw a wavy line around the lid with a pencil. Use a #1 round brush and Butter Yellow to paint the wavy line.

Make Tompte Red dots on border the same way as described above, but to make larger dots than previously use a pencil eraser instead of a brush handle.

Allow paint to dry overnight.

Using a 1" flat brush apply several coats of Matte Interior Sealer, allowing the sealer to dry between coats.

Creamy Curried Apple & Butternut Squash Soup

Curry powders tend to vary in flavor and intensity. This recipe has a mild curry flavor. Adjust the amount of curry powder to your preference. Butternut squash is really good for you; this is a great way to get the family to eat it (and love it).

    1 large or 2 small butternut squash (about 3-4 lbs. total)
    4 T butter, divided
    1 large onion, finely chopped (about 1 ½ cups)
    2 large or 3 medium cloves garlic, minced
    4 cups chicken or vegetable broth
    4 medium apples, peeled and chopped into ½" pieces
    2 tsp. curry powder
    2 T light brown sugar
    1 pint half and half cream

Place squash on baking tray that has been covered with foil. Bake at 350 degrees for about 50-65 minutes until the neck is soft when a knife is inserted. Remove from oven and leave on pan to cool.

While squash is cooling, melt 2 T butter in a large skillet. Add the onion and garlic and cook until soft. Remove from skillet and add to a large soup pot. Set aside.

Melt 2 T of butter in a skillet and add apple slices; cook until soft and golden. Set aside.

Cut squash in half lengthwise. Scoop out and discard the seeds. Peel the squash and cut into 1" chunks; add to the soup pot. Cover squash, onions, and garlic with chicken broth; simmer uncovered about 45 minutes. Add apples, curry powder and brown sugar and simmer another 30 minutes.

Place soup in blender or food processor and puree in batches. Return to soup pot. Add half and half and heat through gently (do not allow to boil). Add a little milk if soup is too thick. Season to taste with salt and pepper.

Makes about 10 servings.

Fruit of the Spirit

STITCHERY

I have framed my stitchery, but it would also make a lovely pillow or would be wonderful as the center block in a quilt. Or, just add a few fabric borders, quilt, and use as a wall hanging. However you decide to display your project, it is a nice reminder of those attributes we should all aspire to.

SUPPLIES

- 12" square piece of ivory cotton fabric
- Embroidery Thread from The Gentle Art (1 skein each)
  - Rhubarb #7008 (pink)
  - Cranberry #0360 (red)
  - Chives #7074 (green)
  - Corn Husk #0450 (gold green)
  - Red Plum #0860 (lavender)
  - Sarsaparilla #7015 (brown)
- 10" embroidery hoop
- Washout fabric marker
- Embroidery needle
- Mat with 8" x 10" opening
- Frame that fits mat's outer dimensions
- Lavender cotton fabric to cover mat; cut fabric 1" larger than the mat's outer dimensions
- Acid-free tape or glue
- Ruler

Instructions

Use a light box or sunny window to trace the pattern onto the center of the fabric with a washout marker.

Place fabric snugly in embroidery hoop. All embroidery is done with 2 strands of thread, except "Galatians 5:22-23" at the bottom, which uses just 1 strand. All embroidery is done with a backstitch, except the dots in the border and periods after "is", which are French knots. See general instructions on page 9 for stitch diagrams.

Embroider as follows:
- Rhubarb (pink): "The fruit of the Spirit is"; scallop on border
- Cranberry (red): Cherries; "Galatians 5:22-23" (1 strand); alternating French knots in border
- Chives (green): Leaf on cherries; leaf on pear; alternating French knots in border
- Corn Husk (gold green): Pear; veins on cherry and pear leaves
- Red Plum (lavender): all other words (love, joy, peace, patience, kindness, goodness, faithfulness, gentleness, temperance)
- Sarsaparilla (brown): borders; stems on cherries and pear; bud at bottom of pear

Remove fabric from frame and remove marker with damp cloth. Press gently on back side of embroidery.

To make the covered mat, place the lavender fabric right side down on your worktable. Lay the mat in the center

But the fruit of the Spirit is love, joy, peace, patience, kindness, goodness, faithfulness, gentleness and self-control. Against such things there is no law.
Galatians 5:22-23

of the fabric, right side down. Use tape or glue to secure outer edges of fabric snugly to the back of the mat.

Use a ruler to draw a line from corner to corner and carefully cut the fabric in the center of the mat.

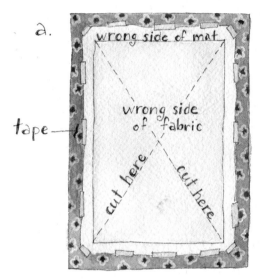

Cut away excess fabric, leaving about ½" to fold over edge of mat.

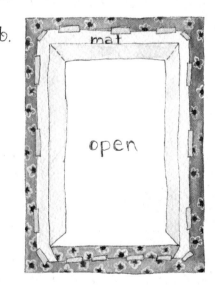

Fold fabric edges over the inner edges of the mat and secure with tape or glue.

Cut a piece of cardboard to fit inside the frame (or use the backing that came with the frame). Center stitchery over the cardboard, wrap edges around to back of cardboard and secure with tape. Trim fabric if necessary.

Place mat and stitchery in frame.

Blueberry Chutney

Chutney is a sweet and sour type of condiment or relish that originated in India, and it can be made from any combination of fruits and vegetables. Serve it along with chicken or turkey—maybe even in place of the traditional cranberry sauce for Thanksgiving (I know- sacrilege!) It can also be spread on a sandwich, or served with brie or cream cheese and crackers as an appetizer.

1 T oil
1 medium onion, chopped (about 1 cup)
1 T fresh ginger, peeled and finely chopped
½ tsp. whole allspice
1 tsp. cinnamon
½ tsp. nutmeg
½ cup sugar
½ cup orange juice

1 T apple cider vinegar
¼ tsp. salt
Dash cayenne pepper
1 T fresh orange zest
½ cup dried cranberries
2 cups frozen blueberries
1 large apple, cut into ½" pieces (about 2 ½ cups)

Heat oil in large saucepan. Add onions, ginger, allspice, cinnamon and nutmeg. Sauté about 5 minutes until onion is softened. Add all remaining ingredients except apples and simmer uncovered for 15 minutes. Add apples and simmer another 20 minutes until apples are soft but still hold their shape.

Allow to cool to room temperature and then refrigerate several hours or overnight.

Makes about 2 cups.

Quilt Label Directions

Make a photocopy of the label you would like to use (you can reduce or enlarge as necessary). Write in the information you would like to include on your label, such as your name, date, city, occasion or reason for the quilt, quilt name, etc. Trace the design (including your information) onto the right side of light colored fabric with a washout fabric marker, leaving at least ½" around the design. Embroider label using 2 strands of embroidery floss (for small lettering, use just 1 strand). Cut the label out, leaving a ¼" seam allowance around the edges. Press the edges under ¼" and hand stitch to the back of your quilt.

Templates

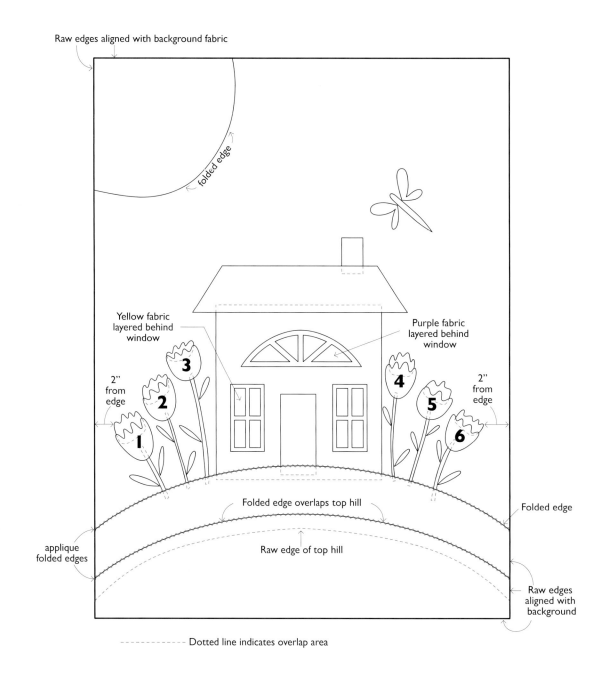

Raw edges aligned with background fabric

folded edge

Yellow fabric layered behind window

Purple fabric layered behind window

2" from edge

2" from edge

1

2

3

4

5

6

Folded edge overlaps top hill

Raw edge of top hill

applique folded edges

Folded edge

Raw edges aligned with background

----------- Dotted line indicates overlap area

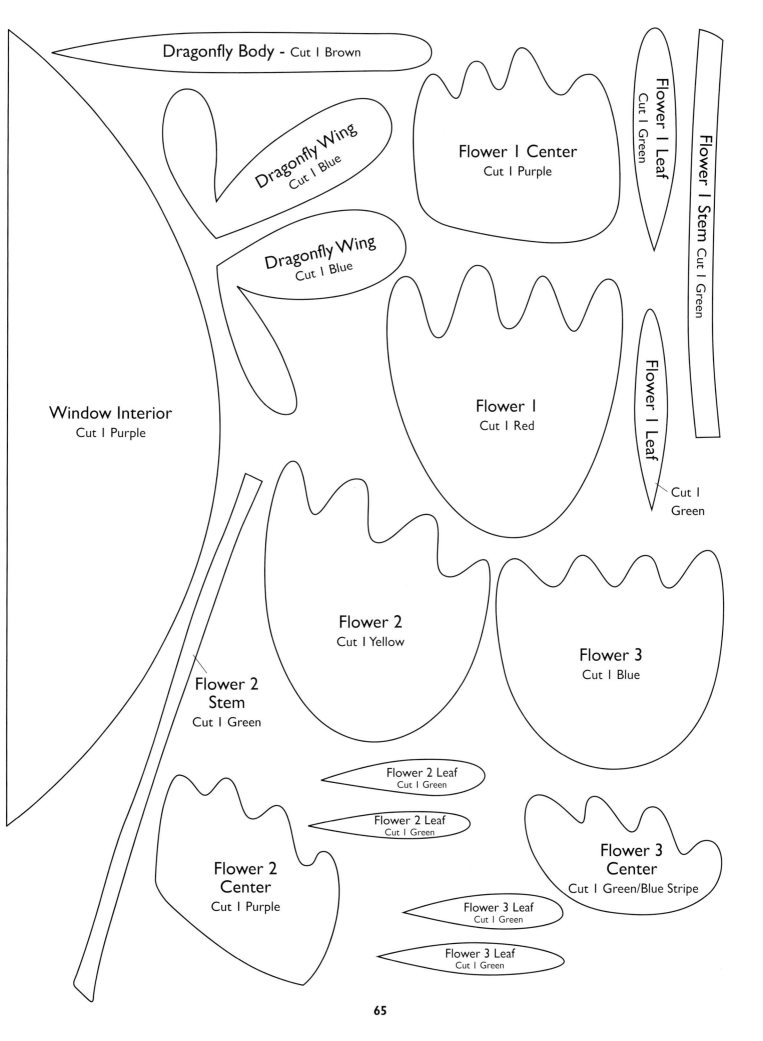

Dragonfly Body - Cut 1 Brown

Dragonfly Wing
Cut 1 Blue

Dragonfly Wing
Cut 1 Blue

Flower 1 Center
Cut 1 Purple

Flower 1 Leaf
Cut 1 Green

Flower 1 Stem Cut 1 Green

Flower 1
Cut 1 Red

Flower 1 Leaf
Cut 1 Green

Window Interior
Cut 1 Purple

Flower 2 Stem
Cut 1 Green

Flower 2
Cut 1 Yellow

Flower 3
Cut 1 Blue

Flower 2 Leaf
Cut 1 Green

Flower 2 Leaf
Cut 1 Green

Flower 2 Center
Cut 1 Purple

Flower 3 Center
Cut 1 Green/Blue Stripe

Flower 3 Leaf
Cut 1 Green

Flower 3 Leaf
Cut 1 Green

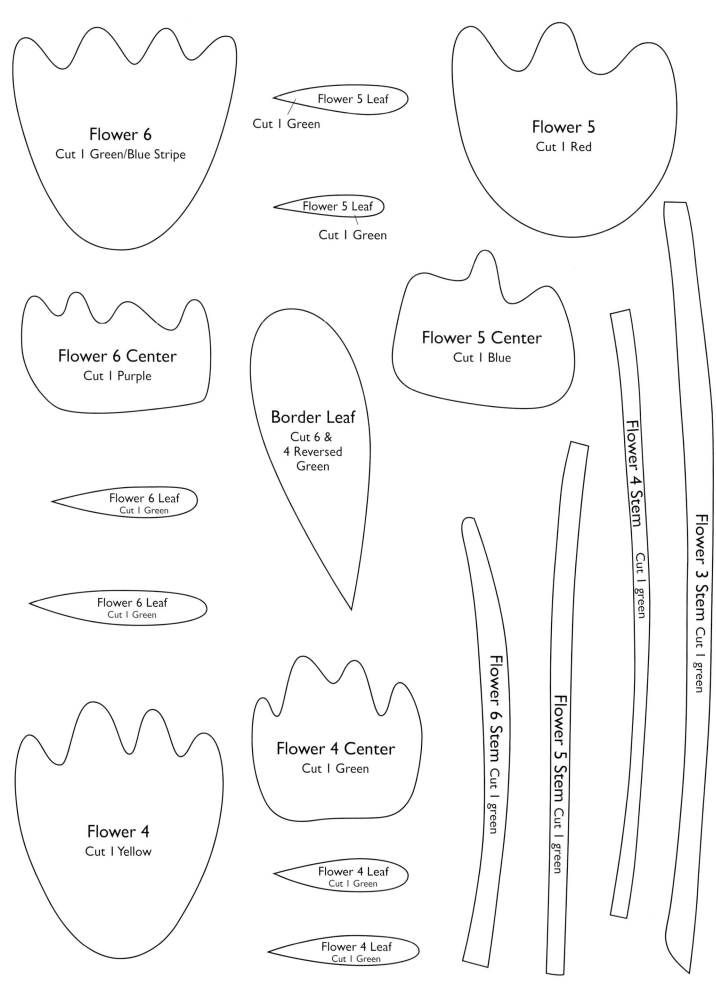

Flower 6
Cut 1 Green/Blue Stripe

Flower 5 Leaf
Cut 1 Green

Flower 5 Leaf
Cut 1 Green

Flower 5
Cut 1 Red

Flower 6 Center
Cut 1 Purple

Flower 5 Center
Cut 1 Blue

Border Leaf
Cut 6 &
4 Reversed
Green

Flower 6 Leaf
Cut 1 Green

Flower 6 Leaf
Cut 1 Green

Flower 4 Stem Cut 1 green

Flower 3 Stem Cut 1 green

Flower 4 Center
Cut 1 Green

Flower 4
Cut 1 Yellow

Flower 6 Stem Cut 1 green

Flower 5 Stem Cut 1 green

Flower 4 Leaf
Cut 1 Green

Flower 4 Leaf
Cut 1 Green

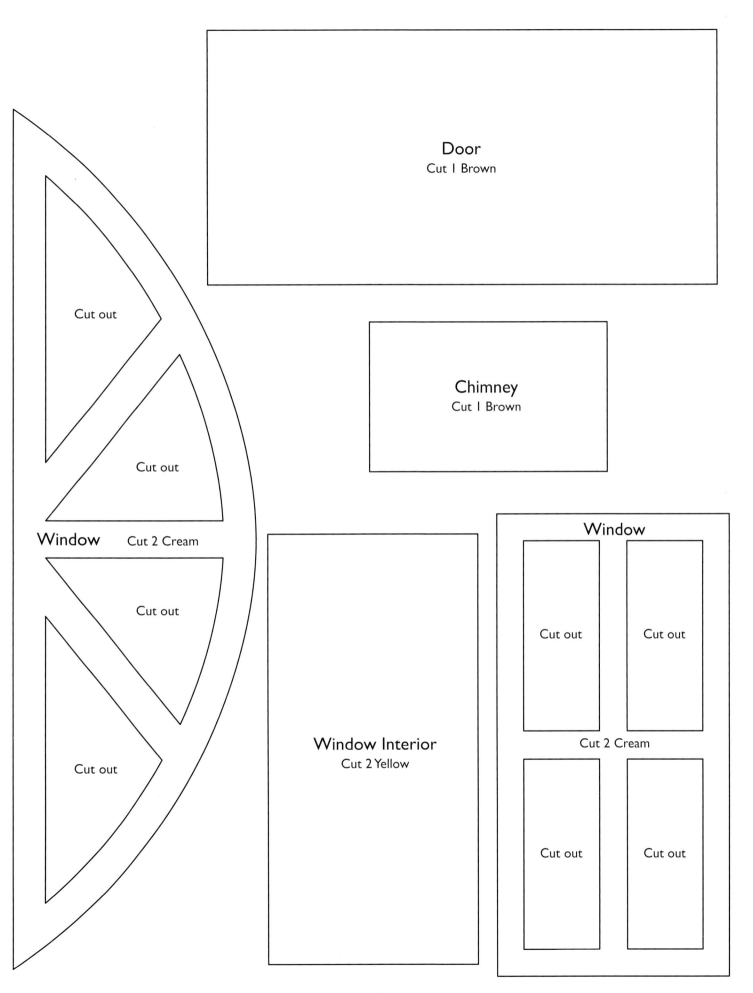

Door
Cut 1 Brown

Chimney
Cut 1 Brown

Cut out

Cut out

Window   Cut 2 Cream

Cut out

Cut out

Window Interior
Cut 2 Yellow

Window

Cut out

Cut out

Cut 2 Cream

Cut out

Cut out

67

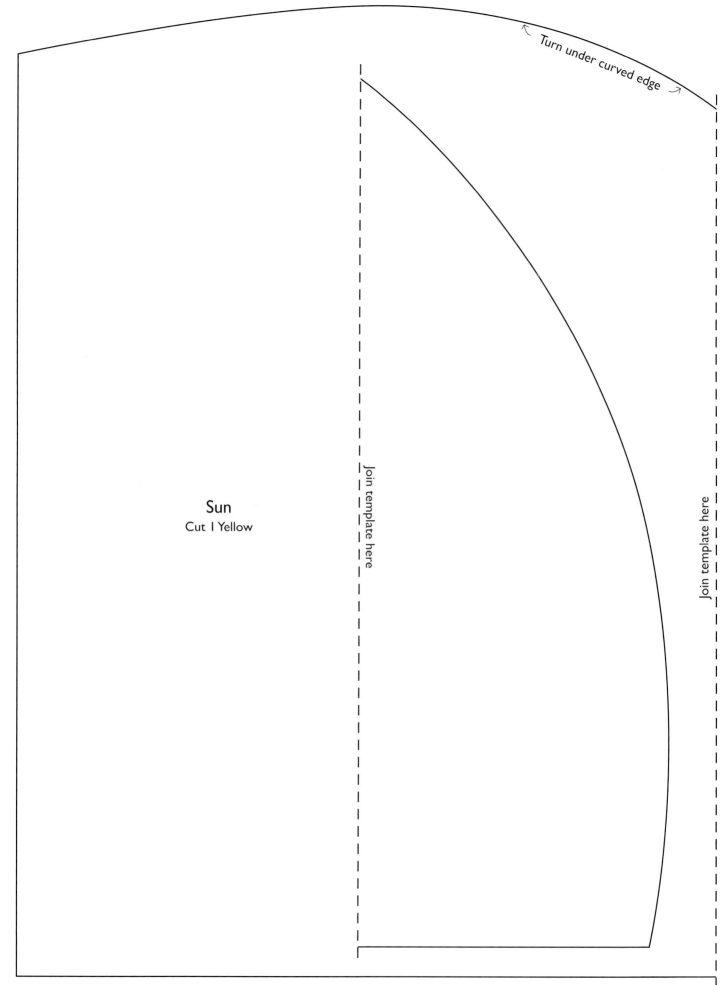

Turn under curved edge

Sun
Cut 1 Yellow

Join template here

Join template here

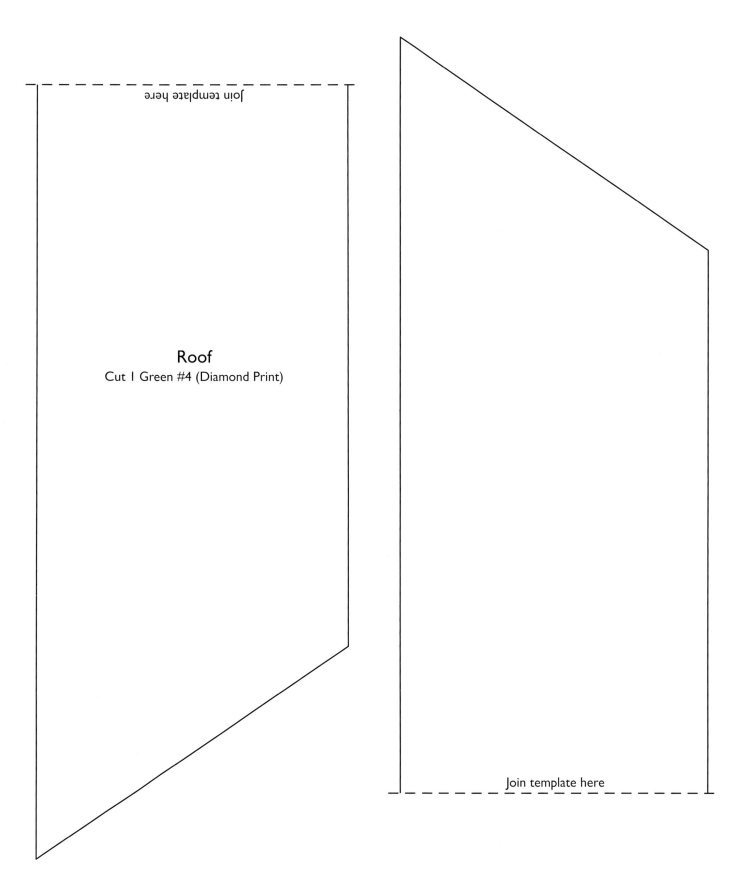

Join template here

Roof
Cut 1 Green #4 (Diamond Print)

Join template here

Turn under curved edge

Place on fold

Bottom Hill Part 1
Cut 1 Green #3

Join template here

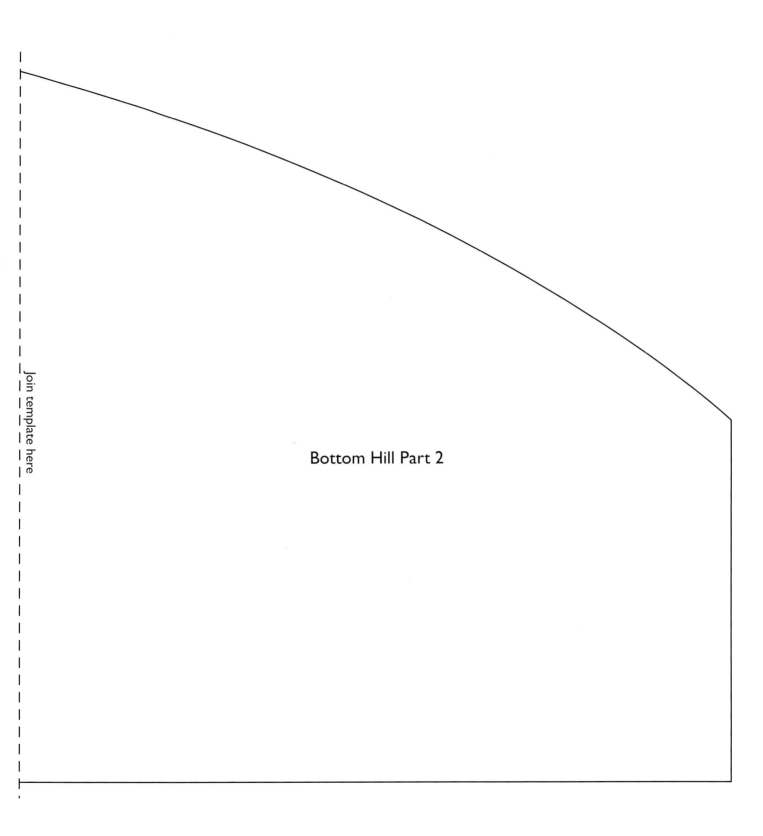

Join template here

Bottom Hill Part 2

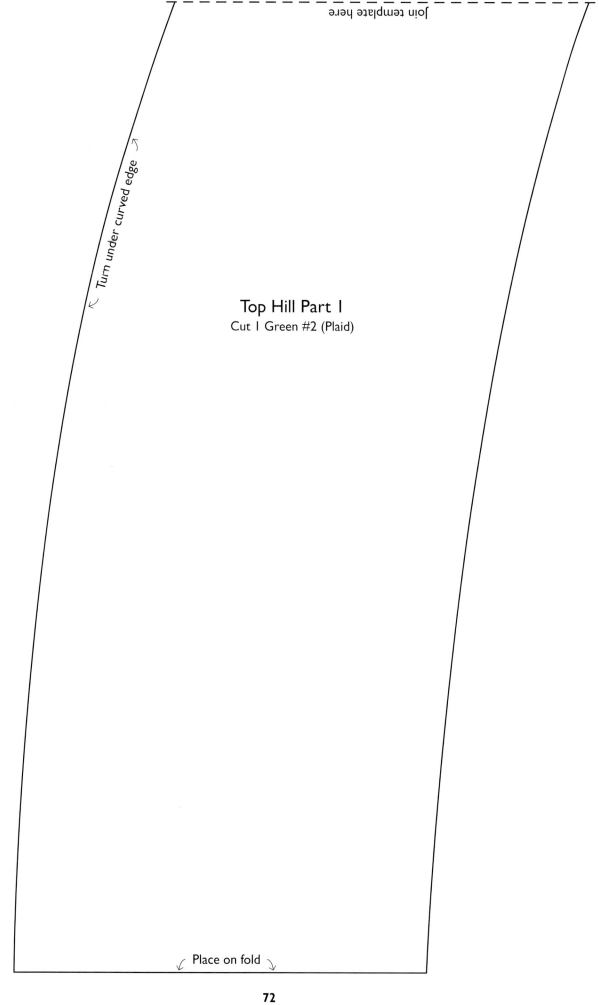

Join template here

Turn under curved edge ↗

Top Hill Part 1
Cut 1 Green #2 (Plaid)

Place on fold

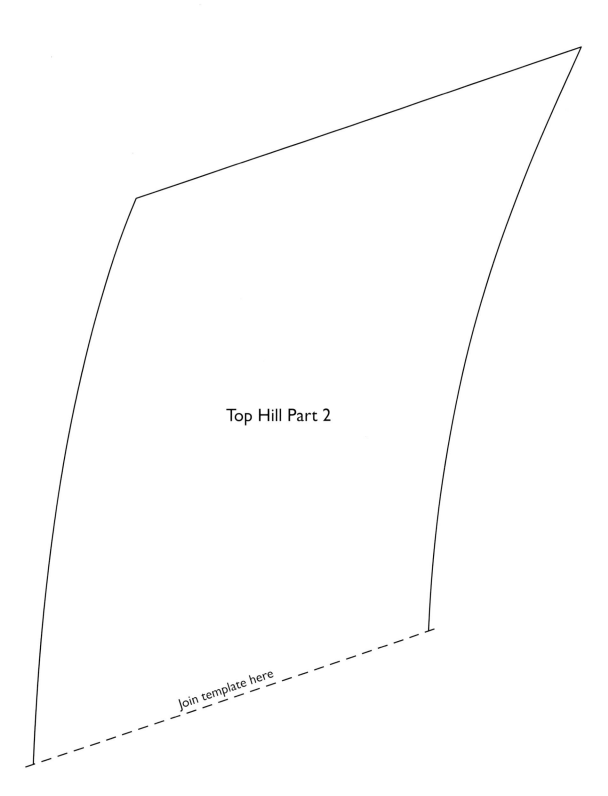

Top Hill Part 2

Join template here

Choose

home is

house is?

Center point of pattern

Join template here — B

s and beams

e and drea

s, ns.

Join template here — C

Join template here — C

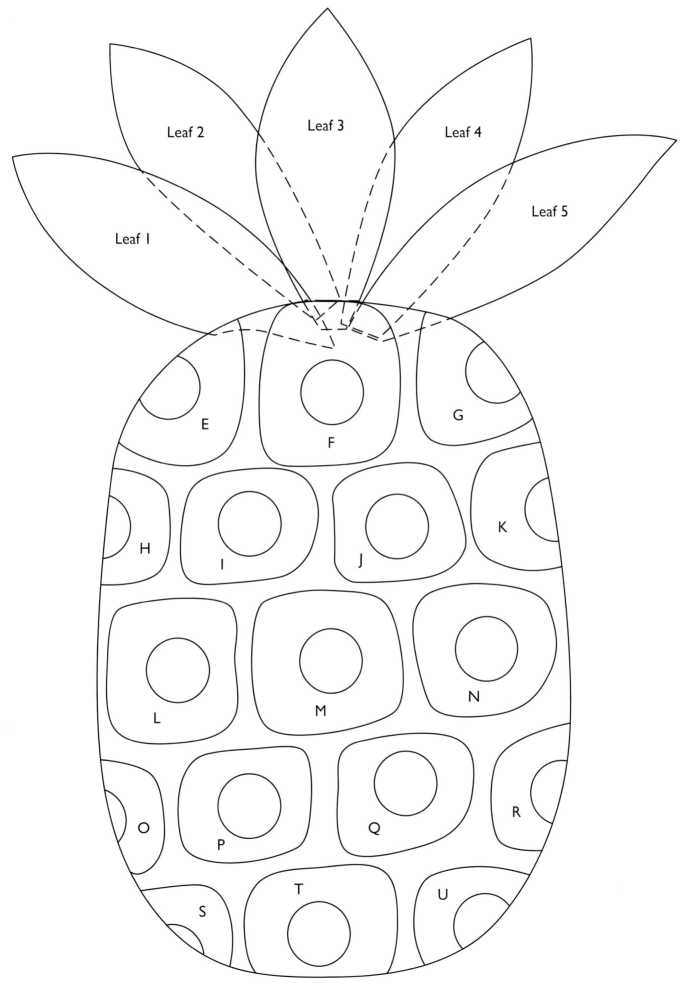

Leaf 2

Leaf 3

Leaf 4

Leaf 1

Leaf 5

E

F

G

H

I

J

K

L

M

N

O

P

Q

R

S

T

U

77

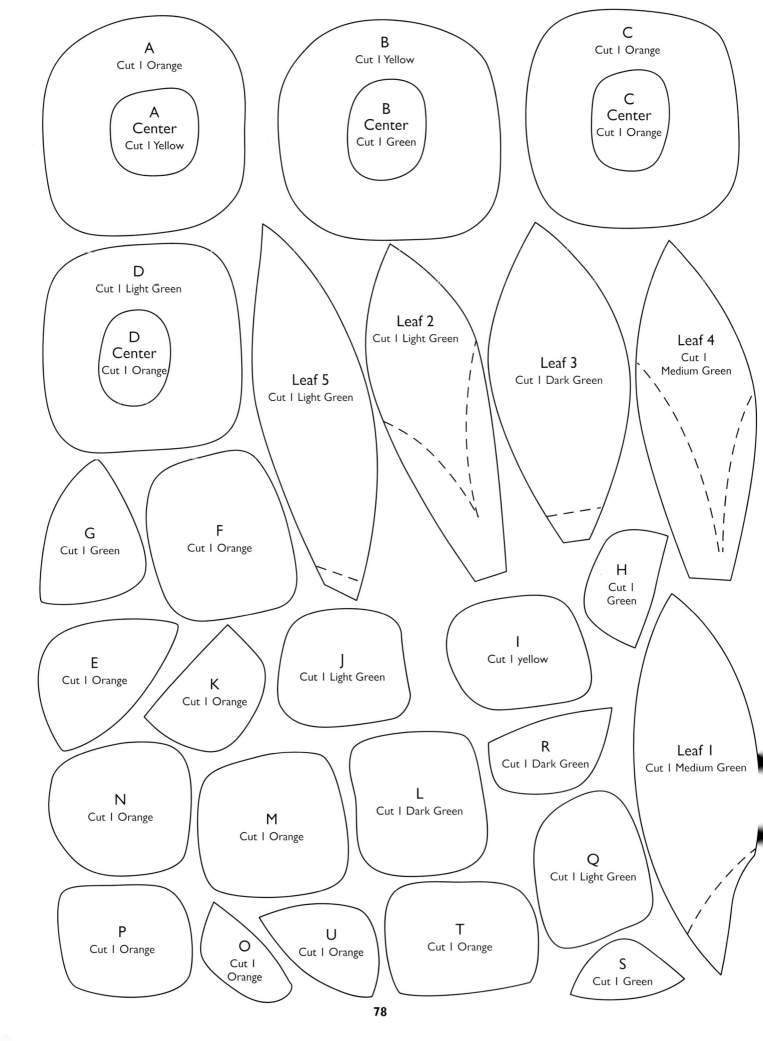

A
Cut 1 Orange

A
Center
Cut 1 Yellow

B
Cut 1 Yellow

B
Center
Cut 1 Green

C
Cut 1 Orange

C
Center
Cut 1 Orange

D
Cut 1 Light Green

D
Center
Cut 1 Orange

Leaf 2
Cut 1 Light Green

Leaf 3
Cut 1 Dark Green

Leaf 4
Cut 1
Medium Green

Leaf 5
Cut 1 Light Green

G
Cut 1 Green

F
Cut 1 Orange

H
Cut 1
Green

E
Cut 1 Orange

K
Cut 1 Orange

J
Cut 1 Light Green

I
Cut 1 yellow

R
Cut 1 Dark Green

Leaf 1
Cut 1 Medium Green

N
Cut 1 Orange

M
Cut 1 Orange

L
Cut 1 Dark Green

Q
Cut 1 Light Green

P
Cut 1 Orange

O
Cut 1
Orange

U
Cut 1 Orange

T
Cut 1 Orange

S
Cut 1 Green

78

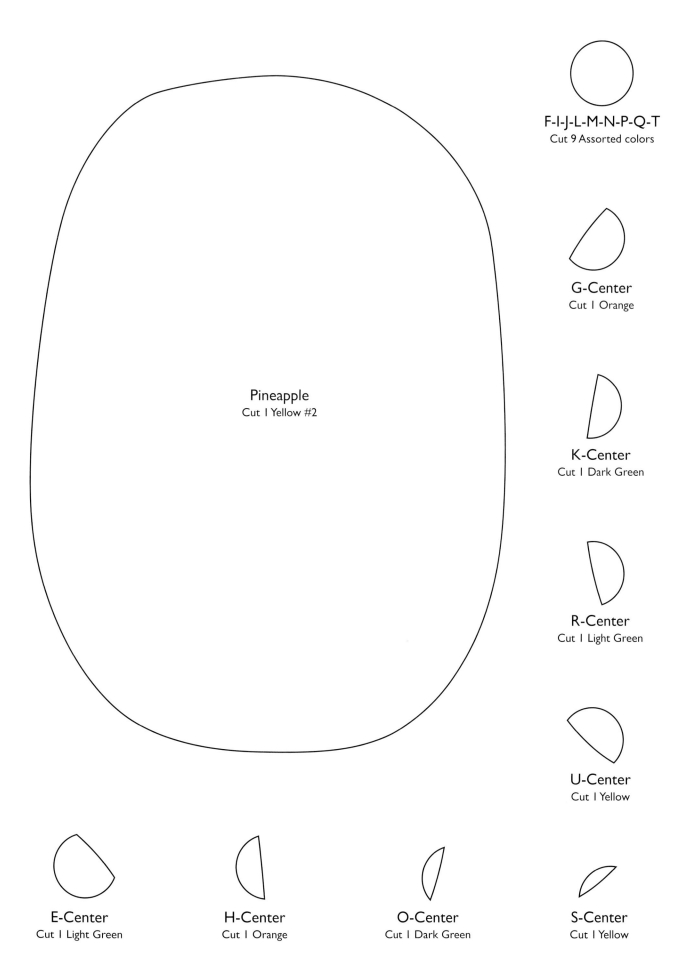

Pineapple
Cut 1 Yellow #2

F-I-J-L-M-N-P-Q-T
Cut 9 Assorted colors

G-Center
Cut 1 Orange

K-Center
Cut 1 Dark Green

R-Center
Cut 1 Light Green

U-Center
Cut 1 Yellow

E-Center
Cut 1 Light Green

H-Center
Cut 1 Orange

O-Center
Cut 1 Dark Green

S-Center
Cut 1 Yellow

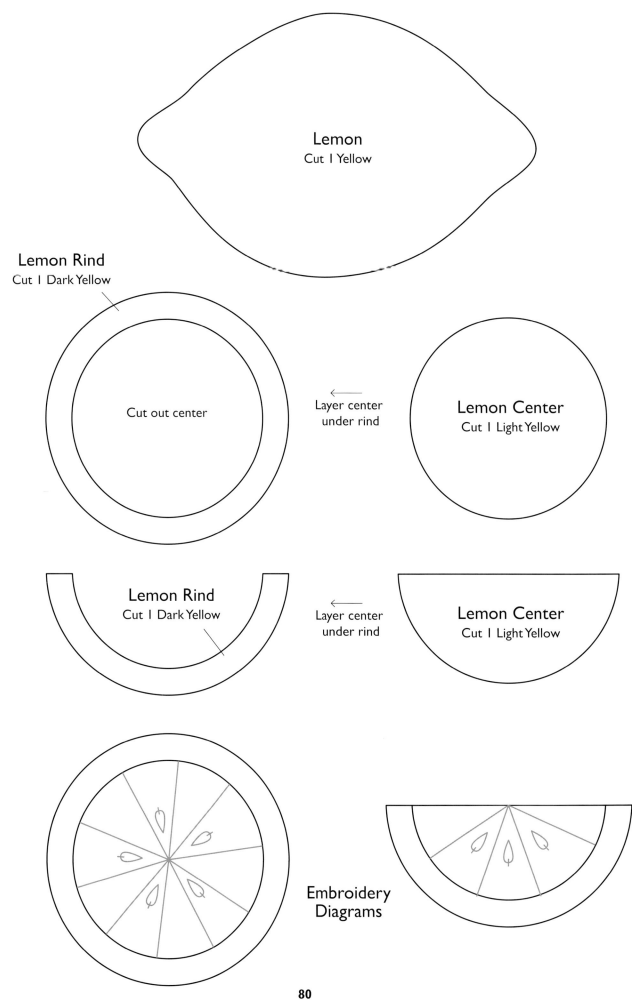

Lemon
Cut 1 Yellow

Lemon Rind
Cut 1 Dark Yellow

Cut out center

← Layer center
under rind

Lemon Center
Cut 1 Light Yellow

Lemon Rind
Cut 1 Dark Yellow

← Layer center
under rind

Lemon Center
Cut 1 Light Yellow

Embroidery
Diagrams

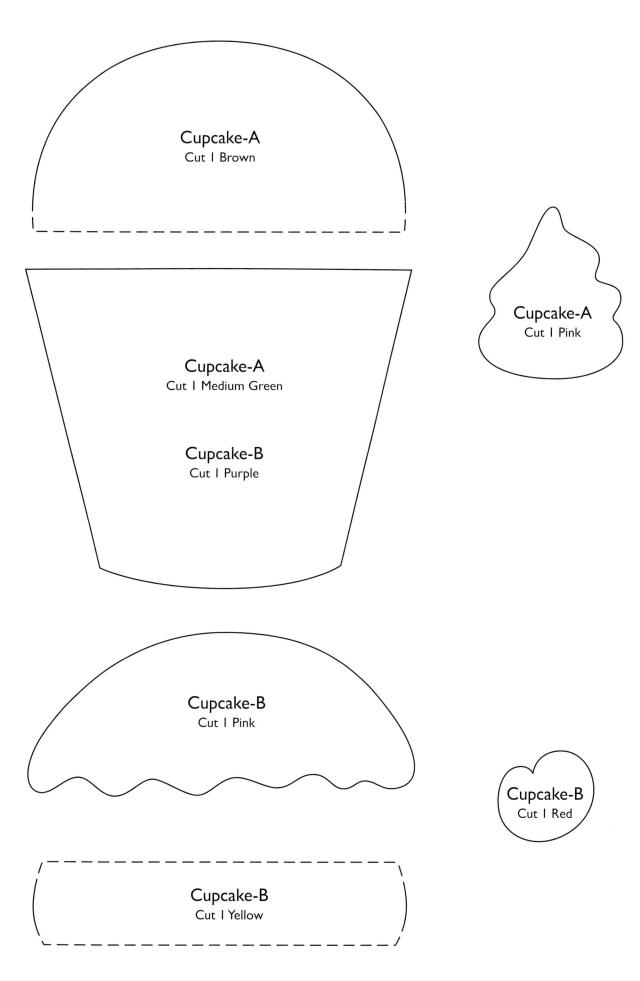

Cupcake-A
Cut 1 Brown

Cupcake-A
Cut 1 Pink

Cupcake-A
Cut 1 Medium Green

Cupcake-B
Cut 1 Purple

Cupcake-B
Cut 1 Pink

Cupcake-B
Cut 1 Red

Cupcake-B
Cut 1 Yellow

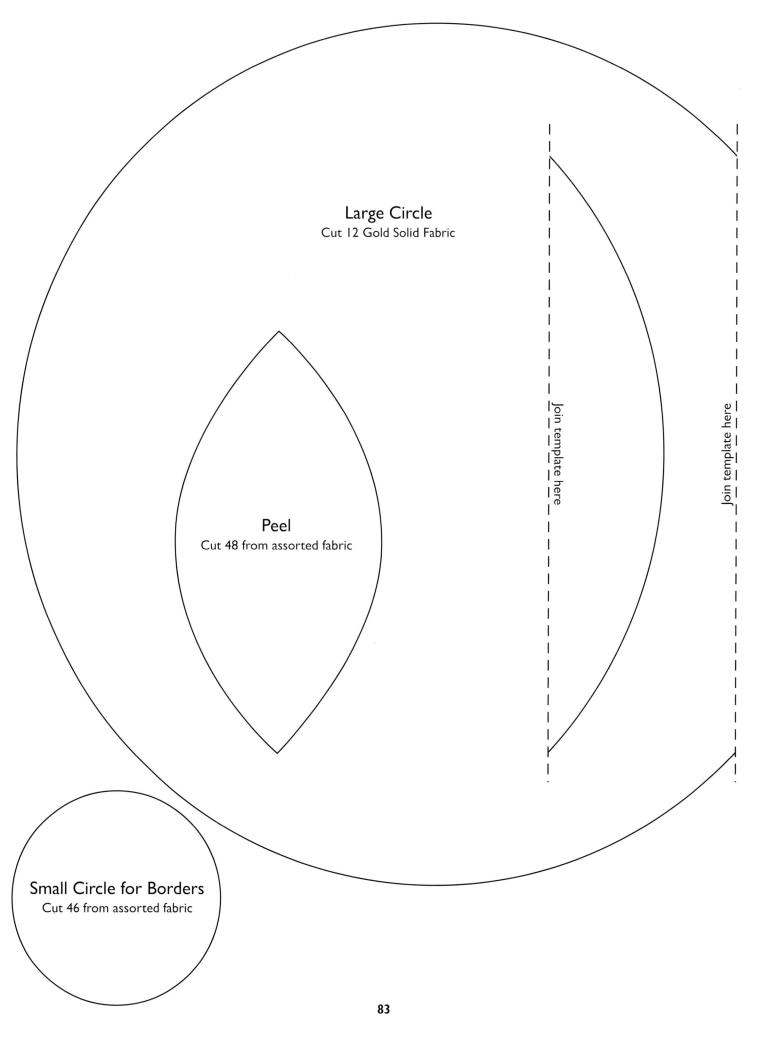

Large Circle
Cut 12 Gold Solid Fabric

Peel
Cut 48 from assorted fabric

Join template here

Join template here

Small Circle for Borders
Cut 46 from assorted fabric

Tag
Cut 1 from Brown Cardstock

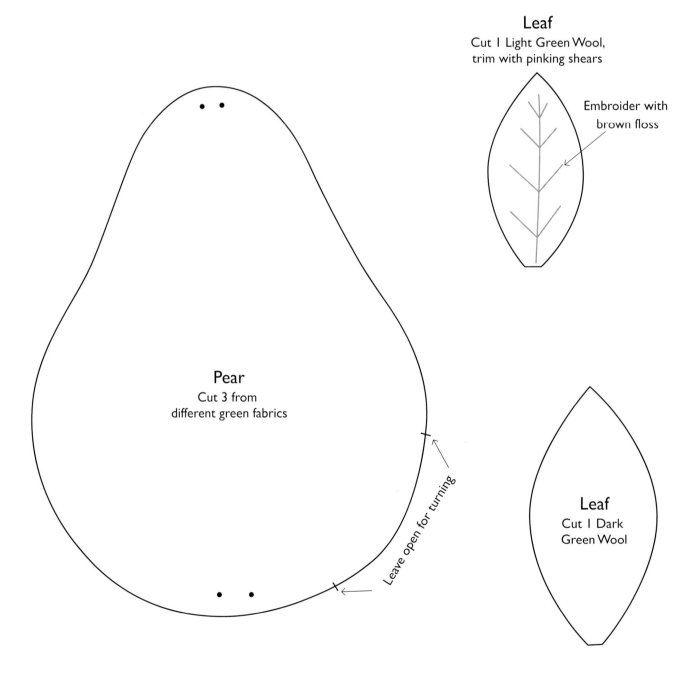

Pear
Cut 3 from
different green fabrics

Leave open for turning

Leaf
Cut 1 Light Green Wool,
trim with pinking shears

Embroider with
brown floss

Leaf
Cut 1 Dark
Green Wool

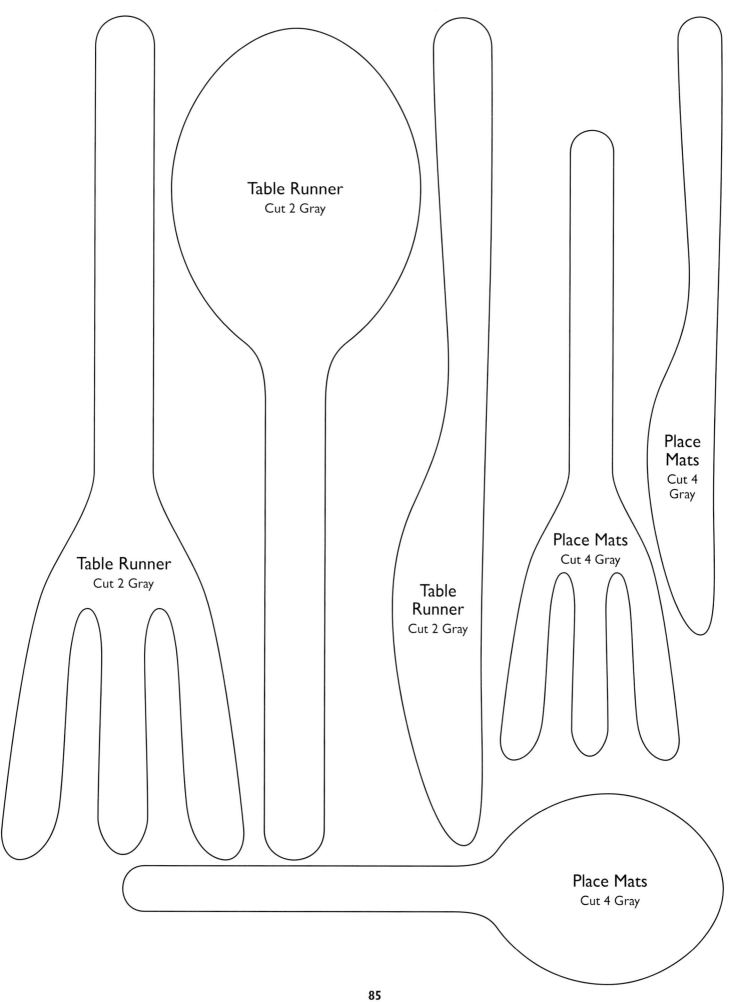

Table Runner
Cut 2 Gray

Table Runner
Cut 2 Gray

Table Runner
Cut 2 Gray

Place Mats
Cut 4 Gray

Place Mats
Cut 4 Gray

Place Mats
Cut 4 Gray

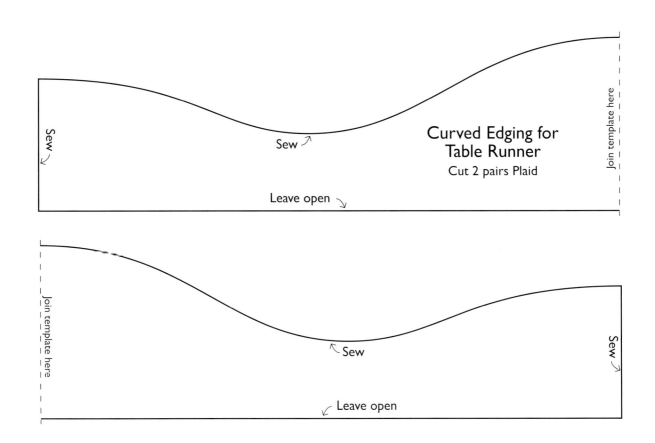

Sew

Sew ↗

Leave open ↘

**Curved Edging for
Table Runner**

Cut 2 pairs Plaid

Join template here

Join template here

↖ Sew

Sew ↗

↙ Leave open

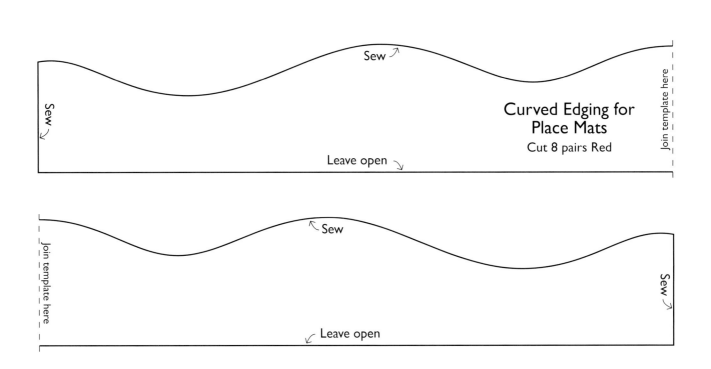

Sew ↗

Sew

Leave open ↘

**Curved Edging for
Place Mats**

Cut 8 pairs Red

Join template here

Join template here

↖ Sew

Sew ↗

↙ Leave open

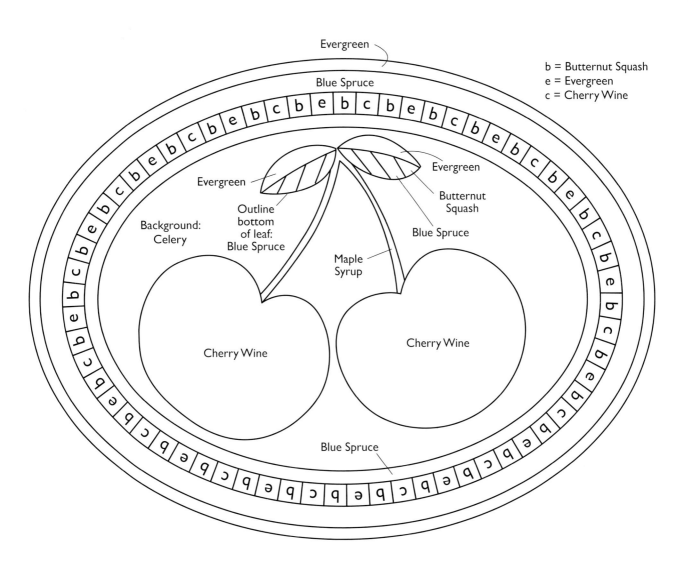

Evergreen

b = Butternut Squash
e = Evergreen
c = Cherry Wine

Blue Spruce

Evergreen

Evergreen

Butternut Squash

Outline bottom of leaf: Blue Spruce

Blue Spruce

Background: Celery

Maple Syrup

Cherry Wine

Cherry Wine

Blue Spruce

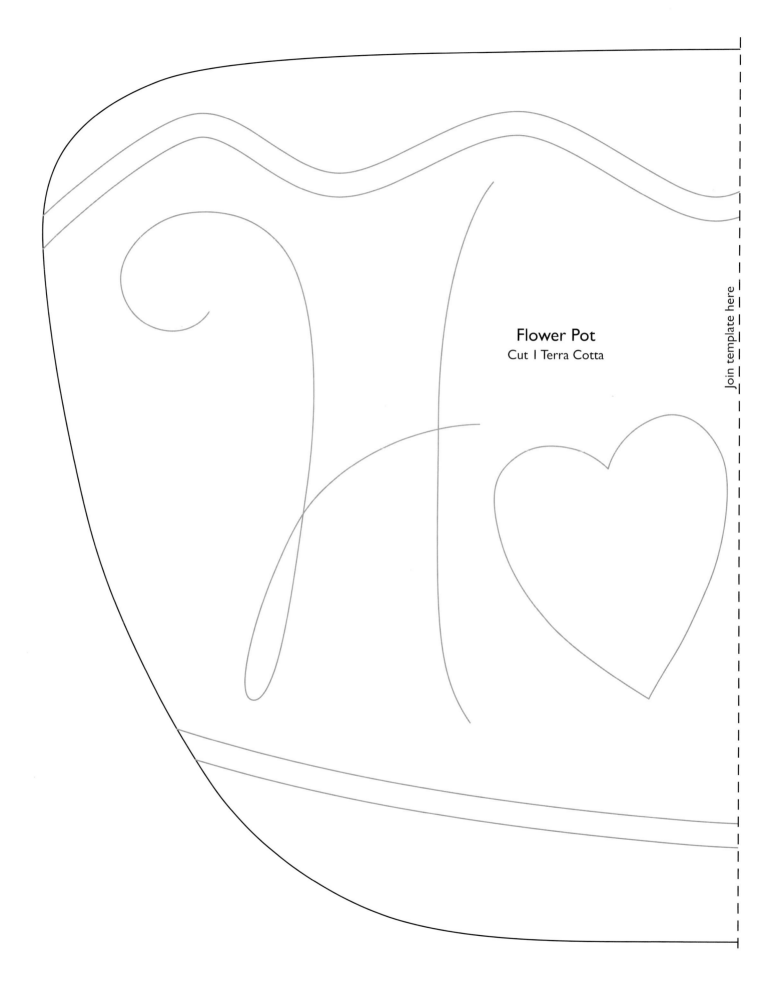

Flower Pot
Cut 1 Terra Cotta

Join template here

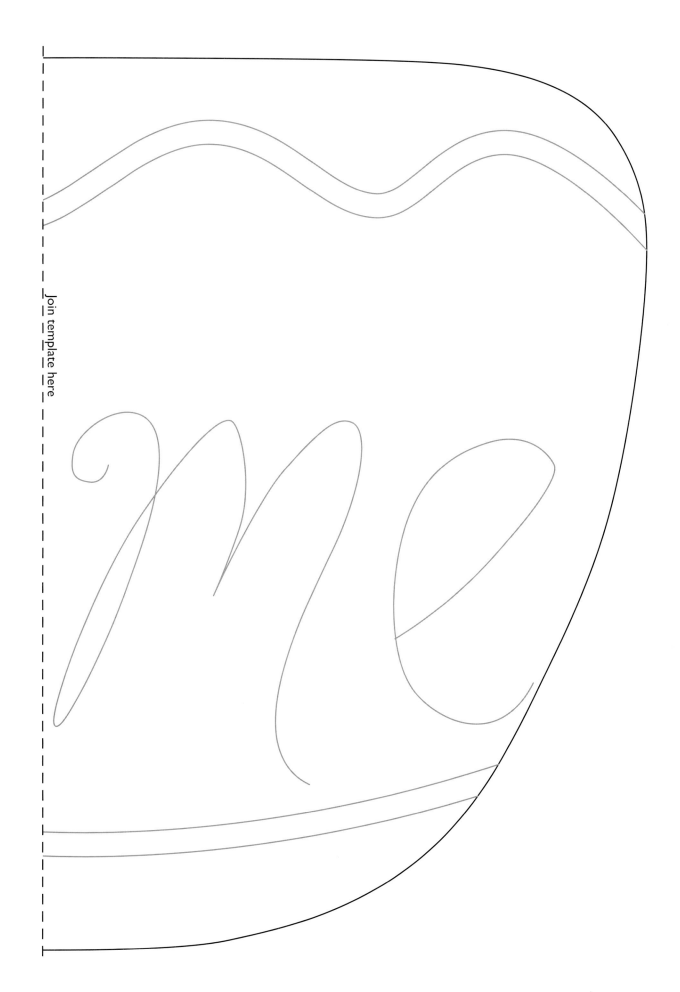

Join template here

Large Flower
Cut 1 Lavender

"O" in "Home"
Cut 1 Dark Blue Plaid

Flower Center
Cut 1
Dark Pink Plaid

Overlap

Bird Body
Cut 1 Dark Blue Plaid

Small Flower
Cut 2 & 2 Reversed Dark Pink
Cut 1 & 1 Reversed Yellow

Leaf
Cut 2 & 3 Reversed
Green

Leaf Embroidery Guide
Backstitch
2 strands
Spring Grass (green)

Small Flower
Center
Cut 2 Green
Cut 2 Lavender
Cut 2 Light Blue

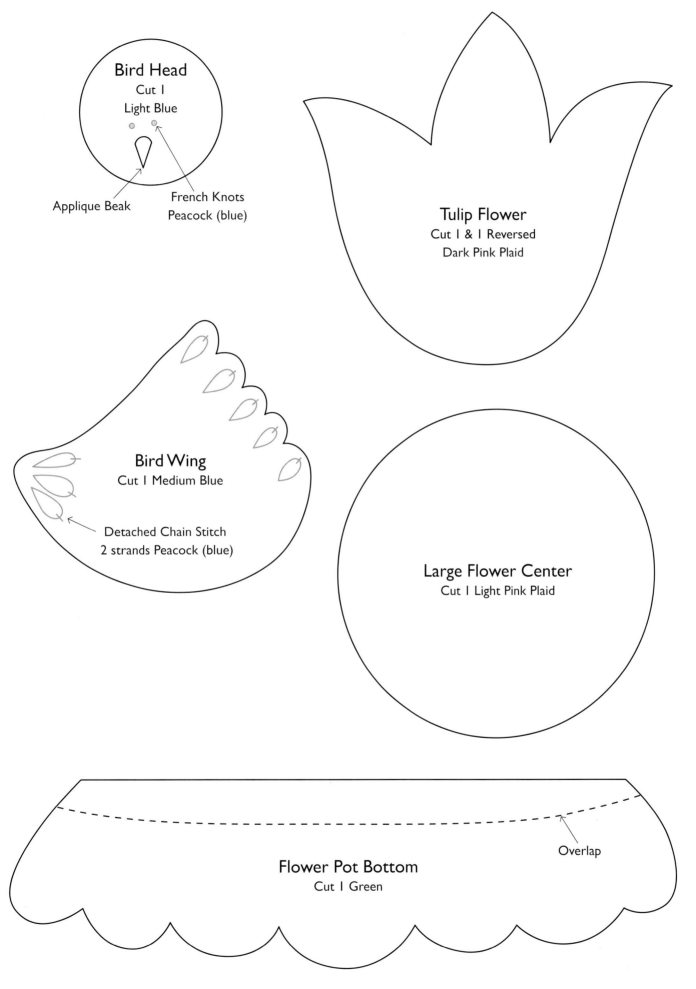

Bird Head
Cut 1
Light Blue

Applique Beak

French Knots
Peacock (blue)

Tulip Flower
Cut 1 & 1 Reversed
Dark Pink Plaid

Bird Wing
Cut 1 Medium Blue

Detached Chain Stitch
2 strands Peacock (blue)

Large Flower Center
Cut 1 Light Pink Plaid

Flower Pot Bottom
Cut 1 Green

Overlap

91

Recipes

The fruit of the Spirit is...
love
joy
peace
patience
kindness
goodness
faithfulness
gentleness
temperance

Galatians
5:22-23

93

love

joy

peace

patience

kindness

goodness

faithfulness

gentleness

temperance